FANFARE

Portraits of The Cleveland Orchestra

FANFARE 🎺
PORTRAITS OF
THE
CLEVELAND
ORCHESTRA

The Junior Committee of The Cleveland Orchestra

with portraiture by Herbert Ascherman, Jr.

ISBN 0-9609142-3-4

Additional publications of the Junior Committee of The Cleveland
Orchestra include the cookbooks *Bach's Lunch*, *Bach for More*,
and *Bach for an Encore*. To order these books or additional copies
of *Fanfare*, please write the Junior Committee of The Cleveland Orchestra, Severance Hall, Cleveland, Ohio 44106. All purchases
benefit The Cleveland Orchestra.

This book was printed by Hexagraphics, Inc., in Cleveland, Ohio.

Table of Contents

ABBREVIATIONS

Because certain institutions are common to many members of the Orchestra, the following abbreviations have been used throughout the text:

CIM   Cleveland Institute of Music, Cleveland
Curtis   Curtis Institute of Music, Philadelphia
Eastman   Eastman School of Music, Rochester, New York
Juilliard Juilliard School of Music, New York City
Oberlin   Oberlin Conservatory of Music, Oberlin, Ohio

Each Orchestra member's name is followed by his or her instrument or position and the year he or she joined The Cleveland Orchestra.

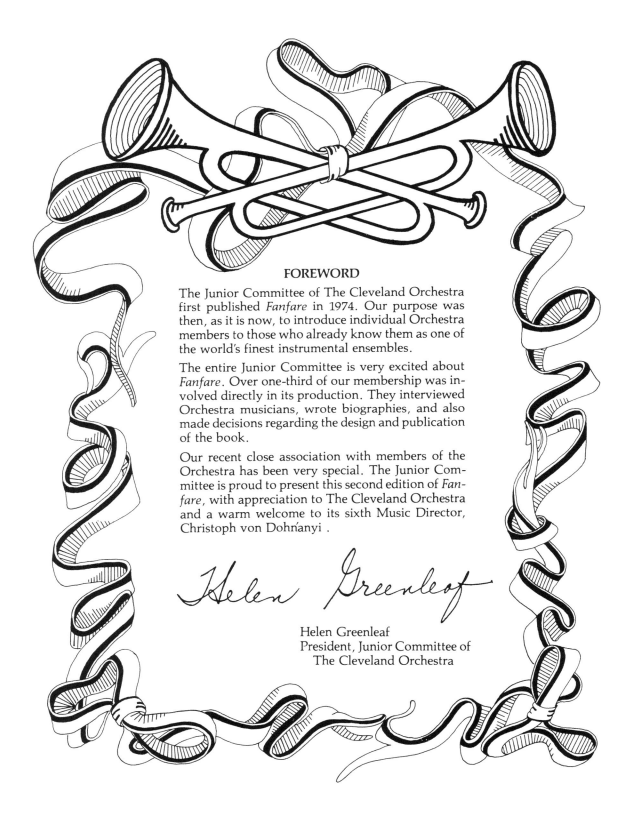

FOREWORD

The Junior Committee of The Cleveland Orchestra first published *Fanfare* in 1974. Our purpose was then, as it is now, to introduce individual Orchestra members to those who already know them as one of the world's finest instrumental ensembles.

The entire Junior Committee is very excited about *Fanfare*. Over one-third of our membership was involved directly in its production. They interviewed Orchestra musicians, wrote biographies, and also made decisions regarding the design and publication of the book.

Our recent close association with members of the Orchestra has been very special. The Junior Committee is proud to present this second edition of *Fanfare*, with appreciation to The Cleveland Orchestra and a warm welcome to its sixth Music Director, Christoph von Dohnányi .

Helen Greenleaf

Helen Greenleaf
President, Junior Committee of
The Cleveland Orchestra

The Cleveland Orchestra is one of the treasures of the artistic world. As *Fanfare* so conclusively reveals, each member of the ensemble is an accomplished musician whose past and present artistic activities are impressive. Yet all the players have non-musical pursuits with which their many admirers can identify. There are parents, photographers, gourmet cooks, tennis players, and hikers in the Orchestra. Some like Alfred Hitchcock, some like Jane Austen, and some like Arnold Palmer. However, with their individual and collective talents, they also show us the sublime beauty and perfection humans can attain.

Members of the Junior Committee of The Cleveland Orchestra provided support and assistance, without which *Fanfare* would not exist. I am sincerely grateful to Cleveland Orchestra members for sharing their time and insights with us. The cooperation of many Severance Hall personnel enabled the project to proceed smoothly, and I particularly thank Kenneth Haas, Jan Snow, David Zauder, and especially Ginger Kuper. Finally, I commend my neighbor Donna Jackson for her help with typing the manuscripts and my friend Thomas Fischer for his help with editing them.

So many people participated in the production of *Fanfare* that it was truly a community project and labor of love in behalf of one of Cleveland's finest cultural institutions. Working with the artists in The Cleveland Orchestra has been an honor and pleasure we always will cherish.

Susan Sackman

Susan Sackman
Fanfare Editor

CLEVELAND ORCHESTRA MUSIC DIRECTORS

Nikolai Sokoloff	1918–1933
Artur Rodzinski	1933–1943
Erich Leinsdorf	1943–1946
George Szell	1946–1970
Lorin Maazel	1972–1982
Christoph von Dohnányi	1984–

Christoph von Dohnányi
Music Director
1984

Music always has been central to the existence of **Christoph von Dohnányi**, sixth Music Director of The Cleveland Orchestra. Born in Berlin in 1929, Mr. Dohnányi grew up in a family that produced several outstanding musicians, the most prominent of whom was his grandfather, the Hungarian composer Ernst von Dohnányi. Concerts at home and frequent attendance at Furtwängler's rehearsals in Berlin shaped the young artist. His home remains very musical, for Mr. Dohnányi is married to Anja Silja, the highly acclaimed German soprano.

As a youngster, Mr. Dohnányi "put little pieces together" at the piano and showed more interest in composing than playing the piano. This disappointed his grandfather, who wanted the boy to become a concert pianist. However, Mr. Dohnányi continued to study piano, as well as flute, throughout the Third Reich and World War II. The era was one of many traumatic experiences and terrible personal losses for his family.

At the age of sixteen, Mr. Dohnányi began to study law at the University of Munich, but turned to music two years later. After winning the Richard Strauss Prize for Composition and Conducting, he entered the Musikhochschule in Munich. In 1951 Mr. Dohnányi came to the United States to study first with his grandfather in Florida and then at Tanglewood during Leonard Bernstein's tenure there.

Mr. Dohnányi returned to Frankfurt and became coach and conductor for opera and ballet under George Solti; he subsequently served as general music director in Lübeck and Kassel, and director of the West German Radio Symphony Orchestra in Cologne. After Mr. Solti left Frankfurt, Mr. Dohnányi returned as artistic and musical director of the opera there. From 1978 to 1984 he served as general music director and principal conductor of the Hamburg State Opera.

Mr. Dohnányi's musical heritage is deeply rooted in the German-speaking music tradition, including twentieth century composers, of whom he is a champion. Among his most memorable musical experiences was attending, as a student, one of Richard Strauss' last performances in Munich. Furtwängler, Solti, Böhm, and Klemperer had the most impact on him professionally. He was profoundly influenced by George Szell, as well.

Mr. Dohnányi's appointment as Music Director brought the Orchestra genuine congratulations from musicians and conductors worldwide. Most importantly, Cleveland Orchestra members and administrators and Northern Ohio residents happily welcome him to a grand music-making tradition.

11

Yoel Levi
Resident Conductor
1978

There was never any question in **Yoel Levi's** mind that he would become a professional musician. Perhaps it was the fact that, at age five, he could recognize each piece in his father's vast record collection, or the time at age seven, when he played the entire book of music instead of just one piece during a student concert, which gave the boy and his family a clue to his musical abilities.

Born in Romania, Mr. Levi moved to Israel with his family as a child. At six, he began to study cello. It was not until Mr. Levi was eleven that he began playing the violin, because he had to return his borrowed cello, and more violins were available then in Israel.

Mr. Levi earned his master of arts degree at the Tel Aviv Academy of Music, and simultaneously studied under Mendi Rodan at the Jerusalem Academy. After study with Franco Ferrara in Italy and Kiril Kondrashin in Holland, as well as work at London's Guildhall School of Music and Drama, Mr. Levi embarked upon a career in Europe.

In 1978 he won the Conductors' International Competition in France. He has appeared as guest conductor with orchestras throughout the world. "Whether it's Lancaster, Ohio, or Washington, D.C.," he says, "I love to give my best and to make every orchestra sound like The Cleveland Orchestra."

Among the many concerts which stand out as special in Mr. Levi's experience are performances with The Cleveland Orchestra of Mahler's Second Symphony and Beethoven's Ninth Symphony and two benefits, one with soloist Leontyne Price and one for the nuclear freeze movement. "Music-making is a paradox to what is happening in the world. Through art we get values and beauty, yet at the moment, everything is moving toward a blow-up."

Mr. Levi, however, is at peace in Cleveland. Living with his wife Jacqueline and their two sons, he feels the city is a wonderful place to raise children. Tennis provides a relaxing break in his busy routine of studying, rehearsing, and participating in artistic and administrative details of the Orchestra's operation.

Robert Page fills a dual role with The Cleveland Orchestra, acting as both assistant conductor and director of choruses. Prior to his appointment to the Orchestra he compiled a wealth of experience in choral conducting. He began by teaching a high school choir in his home state of Texas and progressed to more prestigious positions such as director of choral activities at Temple University and music department chairman at Carnegie-Mellon University.

Mr. Page was appointed director of choruses in 1971 and assistant conductor in 1979. He made his Cleveland Orchestra conducting debut in 1973 and subsequently has conducted often. He also has guest conducted many other orchestras in the U.S. and South America.

Concurrent with his Orchestra duties, Mr. Page acts as chorus master and conductor of the Cleveland Opera, music director and conductor of the Mendelssohn Choir of Pittsburgh, and founder, director, and conductor of the Robert Page Singers. Mr. Page's arrangements and compositions are published by Theodore Presser, Standard Music Publishing, and Associated Music Publishing.

Mr. Page began his musical training on the piano at an early age. His mother served as piano teacher for all ten of her children. Although Mr. Page continued to study piano as he grew up, he did not consider music as a career until his junior year of college. He began his college studies as a journalism/Spanish major with the goal of becoming a bilingual reporter. Instead he graduated with a bachelor of arts degree (with a major in music) from Abilene Christian College and a master of music degree from Indiana University. He was one of the first recipients of a Danforth Scholarship and pursued doctoral studies at New York University. He also holds an honorary doctor of music degree from Beaver College.

Mr. Page distinguishes between amateur and professional musicians in terms of attitude. "An amateur enters a situation and asks, 'What can I get out of it?,' whereas a professional asks, 'What can I bring to this experience?'" Mr. Page is strongly committed to improving the status of professional vocal musicians. One purpose behind the formation of the Robert Page Singers is to offer vocal musicians the opportunity to be properly compensated for their time and talents.

Mr. Page and his wife Glynn, a vocalist, once performed summer stock together in New York. Their daughter Carolann, a lyric coloratura soprano, made her Cleveland Orchestra debut in 1983 as soloist for a Pops Concert at Blossom Music Center. Daughter Paula is a harpist with the Pittsburgh Symphony.

Robert Page
Assistant Conductor, Director of Choruses
1971

Photo by Christian Steiner

Christopher Wilkins comes to Cleveland as the first young conductor to hold an Exxon/Arts Endowment position with one of the top five United States orchestras. His responsibilities with The Cleveland Orchestra include conducting assignments, especially with educational concerts, and help in the production of Orchestra broadcasts that are syndicated nationally.

He earned an A.B. from Harvard College, and after a year in Europe, completed a master's degree at the Yale School of Music, where he drew inspiration and learned conducting technique from Otto-Werner Mueller. He then spent a year at the State University of New York in Purchase, conducting the college orchestra and teaching music theory. Mr. Wilkins' first experience with a major orchestra was as conducting assistant of the Oregon Symphony in Portland.

Mr. Wilkins' interest in music began with piano lessons at age five. He started to play oboe at age eight, but did not consider music as a likely career until his sophomore year at Harvard. While playing oboe in the Bach Society Orchestra, he was persuaded to audition for the position of music director and subsequently proved to have an affinity for conducting. He was chosen by his peers to lead the orchestra, despite the fact that he had had no previous conducting experience.

Mr. Wilkins attends all Cleveland Orchestra rehearsals and performances and conducts CIM's youth orchestra. He enjoys conducting both chamber and symphony orchestras and has composed chamber music. He favors an eclectic range of music for pleasure, as well as hiking and tennis.

Christopher Wilkins
Conducting Assistant
1983

On the average, Orchestra members began to study music at seven and one-half years of age. Three members began at age three, but the majority started between the ages of six and nine.

Music has been central to the Majeske family for generations. **Daniel Majeske's** grandfather served as bandmaster during the czar's reign, playing clarinet and violin. His father plays violin and his mother plays piano. His daughter Sharon and his son Stephen are also professional musicians; the latter is a member of the first violin section of The Cleveland Orchestra.

Born and raised in Detroit, Mr. Majeske was given a drum for a Christmas gift before his fifth birthday. Since his drum was not an appropriate instrument for a family trio, he decided to spend an eight-dollar cash gift on a violin. In 1964 he was blessed with the opportunity to purchase a 1718 Stradivarius violin, once in the Curtis collection.

Mr. Majeske graduated from Curtis in 1950 and studied with Ivan Galamian and Karl Chase. He has done all of his orchestral playing with The Cleveland Orchestra, and was appointed Concertmaster by George Szell in 1969. His solo performances number more than eighty, with Bernstein's "Serenade" and the Brahms Double Concerto being most memorable. One tour highlight was performing the Bartok Violin Concerto at Osaka, Japan, in 1970. He also recalls that when Mr. Szell conducted the Orchestra in Moscow in 1965 the audiences applauded for almost an hour.

Even as a child Mr. Majeske practiced twice a day. He still practices many hours each day, and does not compromise his routine on tours or vacations. He teaches at the Cleveland Music School Settlement and CIM. When there is time in his busy schedule, Mr. Majeske reads and plays golf. When the family gets together, they sometimes turn the occasion into a small concert.

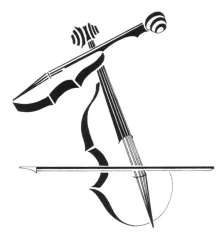

Daniel Majeske
Concertmaster
1955

Native Clevelander **Eugene Altschuler** graduated from John Adams High School. He then attended Eastman and earned bachelor's degrees in both violin and composition, as well as the coveted performer's certificate.

Having served in Army Intelligence during World War II, he returned to music by joining the Pittsburgh Symphony as a first violinist. It was then that Fritz Reiner showed unusual interest in the young musician and took him on as a private student. The next step in Mr. Altschuler's career took him to New York City for private study with Raphael Bronstein, whom he calls "a great violinist and extraordinary teacher."

Before coming to Cleveland, Mr. Altschuler served for nine seasons as concertmaster of the Syracuse Symphony and has held the same position with the St. Paul Chamber Orchestra, the St. Paul Opera Company, the New Orleans Philharmonic, and the Orchestra of Sao Paulo, Brazil. He has performed with the orchestras in Rochester and Detroit as well.

Mr. Altschuler has participated in numerous music festivals and chamber music performances, headed his own string quartet, and appeared as soloist with orchestras in the U.S., Europe, and South America. He was appointed associate concertmaster of The Cleveland Orchestra at the beginning of the 1982 Blossom season. In March and April 1983 he made his solo debut with the Orchestra, performing Mozart's Violin Concerto No. 4.

During more than three years of touring in Europe, he was awarded the "artist's diploma with special distinction" by the city of Basel for his contribution to musical life in Switzerland. Mr. Altschuler has taught extensively in this country and abroad in colleges, universities, and in individual and master classes.

Thirteen Cleveland Orchestra members are Cleveland-area natives, and one-fourth come from foreign countries such as Germany, Russia, Cuba, Canada, Czechoslovakia, and Japan.

Eugene Altschuler
Violin
1981

"Music gives you more for your efforts than any other profession," is **Vaclav Benkovic's** evaluation of his livelihood. He grew up in Czechoslovakia, where his home was filled with dance and popular music. His father played accordion and trumpet and his brother played violin. The young Mr. Benkovic started playing the violin and, at an early age, began attending music school. "Music just came naturally to us," he commented.

Mr. Benkovic attended conservatory in Bratislava for six years and continued his education at the University of Bratislava. His teachers were Viliam Korinek, Mikulas Jelinek, Tibor Gasparek, and Ruggiero Ricci. Before the Russian occupation in 1968, he served as solo violinist in the Slovak Chamber Orchestra.

Thereafter, Mr. Benkovic immigrated to Canada and lived there eight years before coming to Cleveland. He was assistant concertmaster of the Vancouver Symphony and Vancouver Radio Orchestra, as well as leader of the Baroque Strings of Vancouver.

His daughter Tanya began playing the piano at age five and violin at age eight. His wife, also a professional violinist, is concertmaster of the Cleveland Women's Orchestra and teaches privately. "I believe the family must encourage and respect young musicians," he stated.

Mr. Benkovic particularly likes Cleveland's Metropolitan Parks and lakefront. "Blossom is fantastic! The music, people, acoustics, and natural surroundings make it very special for me." His other interests include reading, architecture, and travel.

Vaclav Benkovic
Violin
1976

Judy Berman well appreciates the importance of funding the arts and the existence of arts programs in this country's public education systems. Born in Detroit, Ms. Berman was singled out in her Detroit elementary school class because she could carry a tune, and given her first violin. She initially studied with Emily Mutter Adams of the Detroit Symphony Orchestra. Although playing violin made her "different from all the other kids," she chose music as her major, and attended Detroit's special performance high school.

Ms. Berman also attended Meadowmount School of Music for five summers, where she studied with Ivan Galamian and others from Juilliard. She received a B.S. in violin performance from Juilliard and attended the University of Iowa for an M.S. in violin performance and study with Charles Treger.

Ms. Berman played with the Dallas, Atlanta, and North Carolina Symphonies and was an assistant professor of violin at the University of Georgia, as well as assistant concertmaster of the North Carolina Symphony before coming to Cleveland.

With barely time to unpack, she joined The Cleveland Orchestra on its tours to Mexico, South America, and the Orient. Encountering the various cultures, customs, languages, and cuisines was very exciting. However, playing at Carnegie Hall remains the highlight of her travels.

The Juilliard String Quartet was very influential in molding Ms. Berman's career and is responsible for her love of chamber music. A member of the Coventry Chamber Players, she enjoys the chamber works of Brahms and Beethoven.

She keeps busy with her daughter's musical studies and her son's involvement in drama and the Cleveland Play House. She is also an avid jogger and physical fitness enthusiast, and when she has time enjoys both cooking and gardening.

Judy Berman
Violin
1981

William Brown has always loved music, and it played a central role in his early family life. His father, who taught woodwinds and brass at Southwestern College in Kansas, introduced him to the violin as a first grader. He went on to earn a bachelor's degree from Southwestern and a master's from the University of Oklahoma. Mr. Brown then taught music at the College of Emporia and, until recently, included a heavy teaching load in his schedule.

While playing in the Navy's Rest and Recuperation Service, he met many fine professional musicians, and began to consider an orchestral rather than a teaching career. Immediately after World War II, he began study in New York with Raphael Bronstein. At that time, George Szell was completing his last year at the Met, and Mr. Brown auditioned in his studio there. Both came to The Cleveland Orchestra at the same time.

Mr. Brown particularly enjoys the opportunity to perform "new" music, which enriches the experience of concertgoers. "American audiences," he stated, "are more critical, won't accept imperfection, and always want the best."

Mr. Brown and his wife Marian, a former violist with The Cleveland Orchestra, were influential in the musical careers of their children. Their daughter is a cellist with the Grand Rapids Orchestra and is married to a violist in the New World String Quartet. Their son studied music at the Cincinnati Conservatory. A sports enthusiast, Mr. Brown also enjoys Cleveland theater and fine dining.

William Brown
Violin
1946

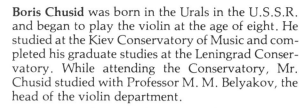

Boris Chusid
Violin
1975

Boris Chusid was born in the Urals in the U.S.S.R. and began to play the violin at the age of eight. He studied at the Kiev Conservatory of Music and completed his graduate studies at the Leningrad Conservatory. While attending the Conservatory, Mr. Chusid studied with Professor M. M. Belyakov, the head of the violin department.

At the age of twenty-five, Mr. Chusid won the prestigious Republic of Russia Contest and, as a result, was asked to play as soloist with the Moscow Symphony Orchestra. Mr. Chusid also has performed with the Leningrad Symphony. He currently plays the violin with the Cleveland Octet and also with his wife, Laura Silverman, who is a pianist.

Mr. Chusid came to the United States in May 1974, and joined the first violin section in 1979. In addition to private teaching, his special interests are bicycling, cross-country skiing, camping, and nutrition.

Cuban-born **Alvaro de Granda** was four years old when his father, a physician who played violin, began encouraging him to study violin. Mr. de Granda's mother was a piano teacher.

Mr. de Granda made his first public appearance at age six. At fourteen he was awarded a full scholarship to Curtis, and he came alone to live in the United States. He teachers there were Toshiya Eto and Efrem Zimbalist, Sr. While at Curtis he was one of the winners of the Philadelphia Orchestra Youth Concerts audition.

Although the Cuban government requested that he return to teach and perform after graduation, Mr. de Granda decided in 1960 to become a U.S. citizen. He has appeared as soloist with the St. Louis Symphony, where he was assistant concertmaster for a number of years, the Baltimore Symphony, and the Marlboro Music Festival, and has played with the Houston Symphony and Aspen Music Festival. Mr. de Granda also has appeared in recitals in the U.S., Europe, and Latin America. Since 1968 he has served as assistant concertmaster of The Cleveland Orchestra.

Mr. de Granda's favorite composers are Beethoven, Mozart, and Brahms. He and his wife Ilse have two sons. His hobbies are stamp collecting, photography, and chess.

Alvaro de Granda
Violin
1966

The number of Orchestra musicians who come from musical families would indicate that environment does indeed play a role in the development of musical talent. Thirty-one percent of the Orchestra members had parents who were professional or amateur musicians. Moreover, thirteen members have children who are professional musicians, and sixteen have spouses who are professional musicians.

Vladimir Deninzon

Vladimir Deninzon
Violin
1979

Vladimir Deninzon was born and raised in the Soviet Union. He came to the United States in 1979, and joined The Cleveland Orchestra shortly thereafter.

Mr. Deninzon's musical career was shaped early. Through the initiative of his parents, who are both interested in music, he, like his older brother, started playing the violin at the age of six. Competing against many outstanding musicians, he was accepted to the Special Music School for Gifted Children of the Leningrad Conservatory. Eleven years later he became a student at the Conservatory and subsequently graduated with highest honors.

In 1972 he won the prestigious Russian Federation Competition and was among the top entrants in the Soviet Violin Competition. Mr. Deninzon has performed with the Leningrad Philharmonic, the Kirov Theatre Opera and Ballet Orchestra, the Leningrad Philharmonic Chamber Orchestra, and the Early Music Ensemble of Leningrad.

Mr. Deninzon and his wife, a pianist, have played as a duo for twelve years. Recently they formed the Severance Trio with Orchestra member Ralph Curry. Their oldest son plays violin and piano. In addition to his chamber music and Orchestra pursuits, Mr. Deninzon's time is devoted to teaching at the Summer Music Experience in Hudson and enjoying his family.

One of Mr. Deninzon's most memorable experiences was a 1965 performance of The Cleveland Orchestra in Leningrad with George Szell conducting. He remembers being moved to tears listening to their performance of *Porgy and Bess* and a Brahms symphony.

Erich Eichhorn's dedication to the development of the professional prominence of The Cleveland Orchestra is evident in his activities on both the local and national level. These include teaching at Cleveland State University, organizing many fund-raising concerts as part of the WCLV Marathon, and founding the Cleveland Octet.

Growing up in Germany, he graduated in 1961 from the State Academy of Music in Stuttgart, where he had served as concertmaster. He then joined the Radio Symphony of Stuttgart as assistant concertmaster. In 1965 he won first prize in the duo competition of the Cultural Association of the German Industry. Mr. Eichhorn came to the U.S. in 1966 and was principal second violinist of the Buffalo Philharmonic and St. Louis Symphony, where he also served as soloist, before coming to The Cleveland Orchestra. He was appointed to a first violinist in 1970.

Mr. Eichhorn's interests are most apparent in his music room. His photographs of his family hang amid shelves of music and instruments. There is ample space for Cleveland Octet rehearsals and student lessons and a corner for relaxing and enjoying the gardens he has planted outside to reap the beauty and bounty of Cleveland's seasons.

Erich Eichhorn
Violin
1968

Russian-born **Samuel Epstein** never considered anything except a musical career. "I knew I would need to make a living and I grew up with musicians around me. My father, brothers, and uncles were professional musicians," he says.

Mr. Epstein began to study the violin at the age of six. "In those days," he recalls, "a violin was inexpensive and portable." As a child, he was not very enthusiastic about practicing, but managed to do so with the encouragement of his parents. Mr. Epstein grew up in New York City and as a youth played in amateur orchestras. He feels they were an excellent experience, and their current scarcity hurts young musicians.

Following World War II he studied at the Cherubini Conservatory in Florence, Italy, with Professor Maglioni. He also worked with Jacob Mestechkin and Illya Schkolnik.

Mr. Epstein spent twenty-one years with the Detroit Symphony Orchestra before coming to Cleveland. He has played with chamber groups both in Cleveland and Detroit. Bach is his favorite composer, because he "feels his music inside." Mr. Epstein enjoys living in Cleveland because it has more cultural activities and parks than many other cities. He and his wife Rose have one son.

Samuel Epstein
Violin
1949

Felix Freilich

Felix Freilich
Violin
1955

Born in Altenburg, Germany, **Felix Freilich** entered the music world at age eight when his parents, who loved music but were not musicians, arranged lessons for him on the violin, their favorite instrument. The lessons were three times a week, but neither this schedule nor the necessary practice bothered him. Participation in the school orchestra and chorus encouraged his ability. Indeed, Mr. Freilich's first solo appearance at age eleven was such a success that his father decided the boy would pursue a musical career.

From this point on Mr. Freilich's education was fragmented by the rise of Nazi anti-Semitism. At the age of sixteen, before completing school, he left home to attend the German Academy of Music in Prague (among its faculty at that time was George Szell). Hitler soon invaded Czechoslovakia, and Mr. Freilich again moved on, this time to the Conservatory of Music in Jerusalem, which had extended a full scholarship to him for violin study.

As World War II intensified all young Jewish men were urged strongly to enlist. A musician at heart and no soldier, Mr. Freilich decided to study the trumpet and mastered the instrument well enough to be accepted as a musician in the British Army.

After the war he joined the Jerusalem Radio Orchestra. He served as assistant concertmaster and was a member of the Jerusalem String Quartet until 1953, except for a year's sabbatical in 1950 to study with Max Rostal in London.

In 1953 Mr. Freilich came to the U.S. with his wife Joan, whom he had met while she was an English teacher at the Hebrew University in Jerusalem. After a season each with the Atlanta and Houston Symphonies, he joined The Cleveland Orchestra. The Freilichs' four children love music.

In addition to his orchestral responsibilities, Mr. Freilich teaches privately, engages in freelance work, is principal second violinist of the Suburban Symphony, and plays chamber music with friends. His violin is a Joannes Pressenda, made in 1843.

From his perspective of twenty-eight years with The Cleveland Orchestra, Mr. Freilich credits George Szell with elevating the Orchestra to a first-class ensemble. Mr. Szell challenged the musicians to meet the competition from other major American orchestras and led the way to the Carnegie circuit. "The New York reviews were stunning and caused each musician to feel a personal responsibility to maintain high standards of performance. And," Mr. Freilich observes, "this pride and personal striving continue today."

The first three years of her life were the only ones during which **Keiko Furiyoshi** has not practiced and played the violin. Her mother's deep interest in music led Miss Furiyoshi to early training as well as success. At age fifteen she entered a musical competition that included the entire Orient and won. This eventually led her to enrollment at the Toho School of Music and Indiana University, where she earned an artist's diploma. She taught at the University of Wisconsin before joining The Cleveland Orchestra and has studied with Josef Gingold, former Orchestra concertmaster.

A confirmed traditionalist in her musical tastes, Miss Furiyoshi enjoys playing the "classical to romantic" range of music. Though her responsibilities leave her little free time, she plays with the Cuyahoga Valley Ensemble, a chamber music group comprising musicians from Northeastern Ohio. This smaller group, she feels, allows its members to exchange and develop their musical ideas.

Miss Furiyoshi also relishes the demanding experience of recording with the Orchestra, when there is no benefit of audience response, and special attention must be paid to eliminating extraneous noises. She has enjoyed touring, and Orchestra trips to Japan have been very special, since her family and friends were able to hear her play.

Miss Furiyoshi is a content Clevelander who likes the city's changing seasons and attractive suburbs. She relaxes by tending her flower and vegetable garden. She has planted successfully some special Japanese vegetables to make her cooking even more authentic. She also likes to cook American food and has ventured recently into Chinese cuisine.

Keiko Furiyoshi
Violin
1970

Aside from her instruments, the violin and piano, the two most important components of **Carolyn Gadiel Warner's** life are her husband Stephen and the Cleveland Duo. The couple is the Duo, which plays chamber music in combinations of piano, violin, and viola throughout the U.S.

Ms. Warner began to study the piano at three years of age. A native of Winnipeg, Canada, she made her piano debut over CBC radio before she was five years old. Ms. Warner's interest in music later led to the violin, and eventually to her graduation from the University of Toronto with bachelor's and master's degrees in piano and violin, respectively.

The single most important event in her study of music, however, was earning a scholarship for post-graduate work at the Paris Conservatory at age twenty-one. She graduated with first and second prizes. Prior to this Ms. Warner spent five summers at the summer school of the Paris Conservatory in Nice, France, also under full scholarship. Before joining The Cleveland Orchestra, she played violin with the Buffalo Philharmonic for four years.

The Warners are avid travelers and enjoy boating, hiking, and camping. Ms. Warner teaches piano privately and prefers chamber music for performing and listening. She also enjoys her duties as an assistant keyboard player in the Orchestra.

Carolyn Gadiel Warner

Carolyn Gadiel Warner
Violin
1979

Bernhard Goldschmidt was born in Berlin and began to play the violin at age five. His mother played piano and his father was a cantor by avocation, hence the musical influence in his life as a youngster was great. Mr. Goldschmidt played his first program at eight. In his collection of memorabilia from his early years as a musician are membership cards for two symphony orchestras in Berlin.

In 1939 his family moved to Shanghai, where he continued to study with Alfred Wittenberg, a master pupil of the famous Joseph Joachim, whose experience and traditions influenced him greatly. During his stay in China, Mr. Goldschmidt played in the Shanghai Philharmonic, performed in recitals, and supported himself by playing in cafés and nightclubs.

Immigrating to the United States in 1947, he studied at the Philadelphia Conservatory. In the summer of 1948 he became a scholarship student at the Berkshire Music Center and the following fall joined the Baltimore Symphony while studying at the Peabody Conservatory of Music. After his discharge from the U.S. Air Force, Mr. Goldschmidt became principal second violinist of the Houston Symphony under Leopold Stokowski. He was appointed the Orchestra's principal second violinist by George Szell in 1964.

In the mid 1970s he was invited to participate in the Casals Festival in Puerto Rico and joined the Festival String Quartet. Mr. Goldschmidt has appeared as soloist with The Cleveland Orchestra. He is a member of the Cleveland Orchestra String Quartet and is on the faculties of CIM and the Blossom Festival School, where he is chairman of strings. While playing in The Cleveland Orchestra, Mr. Goldschmidt earned a B.A. in social studies from Case Western Reserve University.

When traveling with the Orchestra he enjoys his hobby of photography. He and his wife Dorothy have two children, Edward and Rhoda.

Bernhard Goldschmidt
Violin
1958

Yoko Hiroe Moore, assistant concertmaster, at one time conspired with her brother to avoid practicing. Born in Japan, Ms. Moore was encouraged by parents who thought girls as well as boys should achieve. Shortly before her fourth birthday she started playing the violin, and at age twelve won her first prize.

Thereafter she began serious study which culminated in her move to Tokyo to attend the Toho Music School, where she studied with Toshiya Eto. She performed as soloist with the Tokyo Symphony Orchestra, played with the New Japan Philharmonic under Seiji Ozawa, and then joined the Dallas Symphony with Eduardo Mata. She has also soloed with the Tulsa Philharmonic and Oklahoma Chamber Orchestra, although her first love is orchestral playing.

Married to Robert DeVere Moore, whom she met at Yale's summer music camp, she is the mother of a daughter, Mai, who studies the Suzuki violin method. Ms. Moore finds American audiences wonderful and particularly likes playing Beethoven, Sibelius, and Brahms. A newcomer to Cleveland, she is impressed with the greenery, peacefulness, and intelligence of the community. Her leisure pursuit is reading, in which, as in music, she finds much meaning.

Yoko Hiroe Moore

Yoko Hiroe Moore
Violin
1983

Forty-seven percent of the Orchestra members began their musical training with the instruments they now play. The majority of the remaining members began with piano lessons, although one started with the Hawaiian guitar and another with military fife.

Ernest Kardos was born in Cleveland, the son of Hungarian parents. At an early age he was introduced to the violin and to gypsy and Hungarian music. His love for the violin grew. He studied and practiced, and as a young boy was soon playing in small theaters, school assemblies, and ethnic meetings.

Mr. Kardos graduated from CIM and received the first artist's diploma in the violin. His dream came true when he joined The Cleveland Orchestra, and he has been assistant concertmaster since 1947. He was concertmaster of the Cleveland Summer Pops for twenty-four years. He also taught at the Cleveland Music School Settlement for eight years.

During World War II Mr. Kardos toured the war zones with the Glenn Miller Air Force Band. He made several records on the Columbia label, the most successful of which is "Gypsy Magic."

He resides in Shaker Heights with his wife Audrey Regan, who is assistant professor of anesthesia at University Hospitals. Their son Steven makes replica antique guns in Tennessee. Mr. Kardos' stepdaughter Victoria is with the Texas Institute of Marine Biology in Port Aransas, Texas.

Mr. Kardos retired late in the 1983–84 season, after fifty years with the Orchestra. He hopes to spend more time at his home in Port Aransas and return to his golfing and gardening. He plans as well to continue to play his beloved Gagliano and Guarnarius violins.

Ernest S. Kardos

Ernest Kardos
Violin
1934

Joseph Koch remembers the days when low salaries and a short performing season forced many orchestra members to supplement their incomes by selling Fuller brushes door-to-door and driving taxis.

Born and raised in Cleveland, Mr. Koch studied at CIM and Western Reserve University. His teachers include Joseph Fuchs, C.V. Rychlik, and Carlton Cooley. Mr. Koch worked as a staff violinist and occasional conductor on local radio stations WTAM and WGAR, and played on network radio with the Walberg Brown String Quartet.

One of the highlights of Mr. Koch's career was heading a string quartet affiliated with Western Reserve University, which played the world premiere of Arthur Shepherd's Third Quartet. Another was a concert in Buenos Aires, during the Orchestra's South American Tour. He has taught violin at the Cleveland Music School Settlement, University School, and Lake Erie College, and conducted the Painesville Civic Orchestra for ten years. He has been assistant librarian of The Cleveland Orchestra since 1968.

The circumstances surrounding Mr. Koch's purchase of his present violin were unusual. While walking to work one day, he was invited into a neighbor's house. The gentleman played in a theater orchestra and collected violins, but was forced to sell some of them to offset heavy medical expenses. Mr. Koch gladly accepted the opportunity to purchase his 1750 Januarius Gagliano.

Music is a long-standing tradition in the Koch family. His grandfather (who played in the orchestra of Emperor Franz Joseph) and uncle were violinists in Europe. Mr. Koch's son Carl has a doctorate in metallurgy and is a professor at North Carolina State University in Raleigh. Carl Koch and his children play the violin for pleasure. In addition, Mr. Koch's nephew, Paul Bunker, is manager of the Youngstown Symphony Orchestra.

Joseph Koch
Violin
1938

Emilio Llinas
Violin
1968

Emilio Llinas brings a wealth of experience to his position as assistant principal second violinist of the Orchestra. Mr. Llinas began his violin studies at the age of six and played regularly with a string quartet while he attended high school in his native Cuba. Instead of pursuing a career in medicine as his family had hoped, he opted for musical studies. He earned a B.A. in music from Brandeis University, where he was a recipient of the Lawrence Wien Fellowship and performed with the University's faculty string quartet. He then worked on a master of music degree at Wayne State University. His main teachers were Joseph Silverstein and Mischa Mischakoff.

Prior to his arrival in Cleveland, Mr. Llinas was assistant principal second violinist of the Detroit Symphony Orchestra and concertmaster of the Gross Pointe Symphony. He also was assistant concertmaster of the Baltimore Symphony. Mr. Llinas is founder and first violinist of the Cleveland Chamber Soloists and is also a faculty member at CIM. He especially enjoys playing chamber music.

For Mr. Llinas, a concert is a tremendous experience. "In classical music, one can experience a variety of emotions, without the strife present in everyday life." His greatest reward as a professional musician is being part of a great performance. He is proud to be a member of The Cleveland Orchestra because of the high standards of performance the ensemble sets for itself.

He relaxes by jogging and playing tennis, as well as spending time with his wife and two sons.

Kurt Loebel began his study of the violin at the age of six in Vienna, Austria. He received great encouragement from his family and attended the State Academy of Music there.

The political situation in Europe unfortunately interrupted his studies. He came to America in 1939 and received a degree from Juilliard. He further pursued his studies at CIM, earning both bachelor's and master's degrees in music. Mr. Loebel's teachers include Ernst Moravetz, Louis Persinger, Louis Bostelmann, Josef Gingold, and Joseph Knitzer. He played with the Dallas Symphony for two seasons before coming to Cleveland.

Mr. Loebel has been on the faculties of CIM since 1950 and the Blossom Festival School since its inception. He has published a number of articles in journals, magazines, and books. The majority of his time is spent on his musical work; however, he does find time to participate in social, community, and political activities.

Every member of the Loebel family has a career in music. Mr. Loebel's wife Ingrid repairs, binds, and restores musical scores at CIM. Their son David is assistant conductor of the Cincinnati Symphony, as well as musical advisor and conductor of the Anchorage Symphony in Alaska.

Mr. Loebel attributes the success of The Cleveland Orchestra to "a combination of many things: self-discipline and professionalism of the Orchestra as a whole, exemplary community support, and the high standards each member sets for himself."

Kurt Loebel
Violin
1947

Stephen Majeske has come full circle in his association with The Cleveland Orchestra. While growing up in the Cleveland area, he became acquainted with Orchestra personnel as the son of one of its members. After graduating from Euclid High School, Mr. Majeske earned a diploma from Curtis in 1975. He then joined the Minneapolis Symphony Orchestra where he played as a first violinist for four years. Being chosen as a member of The Cleveland Orchestra was a most gratifying accomplishment for him.

Mr. Majeske enjoys working with his father, Concertmaster Daniel Majeske, on a professional level. He considers his father to have had a more significant influence on his musical training than any other musician. His father, his only teacher until the boy was fifteen years old, made sure that there was as much time for baseball as there was for the violin. When Mr. Majeske decided to pursue music more seriously, his father encouraged him to continue his studies with dedication. He still plays for his father occasionally to gain insight into improvements that might be made in his own playing. Father and son also enjoy performing programs together outside of Orchestra concerts.

Another major facet of Mr. Majeske's life is his strong commitment to Jesus Christ. He tries to spend as much time each day reading the Bible as he does practicing his music. Mr. Majeske favors the works of Bach because the composer, through his music, communicated his personal relationship with God.

Mr. Majeske's dedication to his family is equally important. He and his wife Susan, an accomplished pianist, enjoy spending time with their daughters Elizabeth and Kathrine.

Stephen Majeske
Violin
1979

Lev Polyakin
Violin
1982

Lev Polyakin was born in Tashkent, U.S.S.R. While growing up he studied violin and piano. At the age of seven he won a competition for entrance to the Gnesin School in Moscow. A student there for ten years, Mr. Polyakin filled his time with seven to nine subjects per day, as well as three to four hours of daily music. During these early years he often preferred soccer matches to practice.

He was a soloist with the Gnesin Institute Symphony Orchestra at the age of sixteen. After graduation he entered the Moscow State Conservatory. Mr. Polyakin served as associate concertmaster and appeared as soloist with the Moscow Chamber Orchestra under the direction of Rudolf Barchai. He has studied with Yuri Jamkelvich and Leonid Kogan.

Since coming to America in 1980, Mr. Polyakin has spent time settling himself and his mother into their east side apartment. While living and growing up in the U.S.S.R., Mr. Polyakin very much enjoyed composing and singing his own songs. As the English language takes some time to master, Mr. Polyakin has had to defer composing works in English. At a future time he hopes to express himself comfortably in his new language.

Gino Raffaelli always knew he would play his instrument professionally. Born in Chicago of Italian parents, he still speaks Italian fluently. "Growing up was different then," he recalls. "Children could not question their parents. I had no option but to practice."

He attended De Paul University and studied with Paul Stassevitch, the foremost violin pedagogue in Chicago whose students have become prominent participants in symphonies throughout the United States. He also studied with Ivan Galamian in Meadowmount, New York. Before joining The Cleveland Orchestra Mr. Raffaelli played with the Houston and St. Louis Symphonies and served as assistant concertmaster of the St. Louis Sinfonietta. His instrument is a 1726 Matteo Gofriller violin. He also plays the viola.

Mr. Raffaelli's most exciting and nerve-wracking experience as a professional musician occurred in 1981 when he performed as a recitalist at Carnegie Recital Hall. Together with Lois Rova Ozanich of Kent State University, he presented a program which included the first New York performance of George Walker's Sonata No. 2 for Violin and Piano. The duo has recorded the sonata for the Orion label, and it is scheduled to be released in 1984.

Mr. Raffaelli would like to be viewed as a musician with serious concerns for world issues as well as for his career. In this regard he co-chairs, with Orchestra member Diane Mather, Musicians Against Nuclear Arms (MANA). MANA is an organization of musicians seeking to underwrite, through performances, the efforts of local groups working to bring about a freeze in the nuclear arms race.

Mr. Raffaelli lives in Cleveland Heights with his teenage daughter Gia, who plays the piano.

Gino Raffaelli
Violin
1957

Besides his interest in physical fitness, **Leonard Samuels** is a theater and modern jazz buff and enjoys performing with chamber groups. He was a member of the University of Illinois Graduate Quartet and also participated in the Summer Music Festivals of Marlboro, Vermont, and Aspen, Colorado. In association with his colleagues in The Cleveland Orchestra, he played with the Koch Quartet and Concord Trio. Before joining The Cleveland Orchestra, Mr. Samuels was a member of the Kansas City Philharmonic and the New Orleans Symphony.

Mr. Samuels has always felt the joy and magic of music. He has been involved in teaching since graduate school, and, as well as performing, finds teaching a perfect tool to convey his enthusiasm to the young people under his tutelage. He has taught at the University of North Carolina, the Cleveland Music School Settlement, and the Summer Music Experience in Hudson.

Mr. Samuels studied at CIM, and received his bachelor and master of music degrees from the University of Illinois. He furthered his musical studies and chamber music activity in London, England.

Mr. Samuels and his wife are interested in Oriental art, especially as it applies to Mrs. Samuels' art work as a designer of macramé necklaces. They have two sons.

Leonard Samuels
Violin
1957

Many Orchestra members are involved in musical pursuits outside their Orchestra commitments. Forty-five percent perform in smaller ensembles, and fifty-seven percent currently teach.

Elmer Setzer
Violin
1949

Elmer Setzer's family is a musical one. His wife Marie is also a violinist with The Cleveland Orchestra. Their son Philip, a violinist, is a member of the Emerson String Quartet, and their younger son Marc is now active as a choral director in Charlotte, North Carolina.

Mr. Setzer, a Floridian, first studied the violin with George Orner, whom he credits with inspiring and encouraging him during his formative years. He attended the University of Florida and later continued his studies as a scholarship student at the Peabody Conservatory of Music in Baltimore. While there he studied violin with Frank Gittleson and Oscar Shumsky and chamber music with Diran Alexanian.

Mr. Setzer played with the Baltimore Symphony during his student years and, after four years of military service, returned to the Baltimore Symphony. He was assistant principal second violinist there until he joined The Cleveland Orchestra. He has held the same position in the Orchestra since 1951.

Mr. Setzer was for many years a member of the Symphonia String Quartet, which recorded pianist Glenn Gould's string quartet, and has performed on Canadian television with Mr. Gould. Mr. Setzer is a faculty member of the Cleveland Music School Settlement.

Marie Setzer's first instrument was an improvised violin consisting of two sticks. Her father, Leonard DeMaria, a violinist and conductor, encouraged her musical interest with lessons and a real violin. After studying in her native Philadelphia with Sasha Jacobinoff, she was accepted as a scholarship student at the Peabody Conservatory of Music in Baltimore. She studied violin with Frank Gittleson and Oscar Shumsky and chamber music with Diran Alexanian. While at Peabody she met her husband Elmer, and both joined the Baltimore Symphony.

Mrs. Setzer moved to Cleveland with her husband, who joined the Orchestra in 1949. During her first twelve years in Cleveland, she kept busy caring for their two sons and her husband, played chamber music, and was an active member of the Cleveland Chamber Players.

In 1961 Mrs. Setzer joined The Cleveland Orchestra as a last-minute substitute and played the entire season. After a successful audition for George Szell, she became a permanent member of the Orchestra.

Mrs. Setzer's many interests include cooking, collecting cookbooks, drawing and painting, and travel. She is also an opera fan.

The Setzers' sons have paid the ultimate compliment to their parents by becoming professional musicians. Philip, a violinist, performed as soloist with The Cleveland Orchestra at age fourteen and is now a member of the Emerson Quartet. Marc is a choral director in Charlotte, North Carolina.

Marie Setzer

Marie Setzer
Violin
1961

Chicago-born **Bert Siegel** has spent some forty years as a professional musician. He began his career in the popular field in order to support his schooling at the American Conservatory of Music, Chicago Musical College, and DePaul University. His teachers were Henri Hayza, a Sevcik and Flesch disciple, and Paul Stassevitch, an assistant to Leopold Auer. Later teachers included Nathan Goldstein and Stephan Staryk. He acquired additional special orchestral training in the Chicago Civic Orchestra, the training orchestra of the Chicago Symphony Orchestra.

In 1950 Mr. Siegel joined the Fort Wayne Philharmonic and, two years later, the New Orleans Philharmonic. Following a year as concertmaster simultaneously of two orchestras in Medellin, Colombia, he was engaged by the St. Louis Symphony. There he met his wife-to-be, Joan (also a Cleveland Orchestra violinist), and toured several years as assistant concertmaster of the St. Louis Sinfonietta. Five years later he was invited to join the Pittsburgh Symphony where he served as an assistant concertmaster, a post he also held with the Pittsburgh Opera and Chicago's Grant Park Symphony for several summer seasons.

Mr. Siegel plays the oldest violin in The Cleveland Orchestra, a J. B. Rogeri, made in 1691. He also performs with bows made by Dominique, Charles, and Francois Pecatte. Since 1975 he has been on the violin faculty of the Cleveland Music School Settlement and is active in all forms of chamber music.

Among his nonprofessional interests are jogging, photography, travel, and woodworking.

Bert Siegel
Violin
1965

Joan Siegel began her study of music at age seven when her father started to teach her piano. A year later she changed to the violin.

Mrs. Siegel holds a bachelor's degree from the University of Denver and a master's from the Manhattan School of Music, where she studied violin with Walter Eisenberg and Raphael Bronstein. While still attending school, she taught violin at the University of Denver and played in the Denver Symphony, where she also appeared as soloist. She was later a member of the St. Louis Symphony, where she met her husband, Bert, and soon after they joined the Pittsburgh Symphony. In off-symphony seasons she usually taught classroom music in public schools, but sometimes found herself in a kindergarten or English literature class.

Her violin is a Nicolaus Gagliano, made in 1772. Inside is a Latin prayer, which can be found only in his best instruments. Mrs. Siegel admits that she prefers playing the traditional classics rather than contemporary music, and her favorite composers are Bach, Mozart, and Beethoven.

One of her most memorable experiences was performing the Schubert Octet under George Szell's direction in 1965. She currently plays with various chamber music ensembles and serves as president of a professional music sorority. She enjoys gardening and cooking and recently has completed work, with her husband, on their Rocky Mountain vacation home.

Joan Siegel
Violin
1965

On one of his childhood visits to his grandfather, a carpenter, young **Nathan Snader** picked up two sticks and pretended to play the violin. Not long afterwards his parents bought him a real violin.

When he was twelve Mr. Snader began eight years of formal musical education at Curtis. He studied violin as well as conducting, primarily with Lea Luboshutz, the mother of Boris Goldovsky.

During World War II, Mr. Snader stopped playing for five years while he served as a combat officer in the Philippines, the South Pacific, and Korea. He was awarded the Silver Star for gallantry in action. After the war he resumed his career, playing with the National Symphony in Washington, D.C., and the Philadelphia Orchestra. Mr. Snader was also a member of the Chicago Symphony Orchestra under Fritz Reiner. He was highly impressed with the maestro, and feels that Mr. Reiner taught him everything he knows about orchestral playing.

A native of Philadelphia, Mr. Snader now feels Cleveland is his home. His wife Claire is a dancer, and their young daughter Johanna enjoys dancing and already plays a small violin. A teacher at the Cleveland Music School Settlement, Mr. Snader always advises his students to practice as though they are playing a concert.

Mr. Snader had a unique experience while touring with the Orchestra years ago in Austria. In a temple in Vienna he began chatting with a stranger, who turned out to be a cousin from Pittsburgh whom he had never met! They now keep in close touch.

Nathan Snader
Violin
1968

Roberta Strawn began her study of music at the age of six in Cleveland. She started with the piano, because her first love, the violin, was too large for her. As a young child Miss Strawn often pretended to play the violin with drumsticks. Her love of music was fostered by her parents, who were both musically talented. With their encouragement, she learned to play the violin, piano, and flute.

Miss Strawn performed with the Children's Chorus, the Cleveland Children's Orchestra, and played chamber music at the age of eleven. She studied at CIM with Margaret Randall, whom she credits as being an exceptionally fine teacher. Upon graduation, Miss Strawn went to New York City to work on a master's degree. While in New York, she was called to audition for The Cleveland Orchestra. Miss Strawn, at the age of twenty-two, joined the Orchestra during the Szell era.

She has been a member of the Severance String Quartet and also served on the faculty of the Colorado College Summer Festival. She has performed widely with orchestras throughout Ohio.

Miss Strawn enjoys reading and cooking in her spare time and relaxes to jazz. As for the city of Cleveland, she comments, "I was born here and have lived here all my life. I love it . . . besides, we have The Cleveland Orchestra."

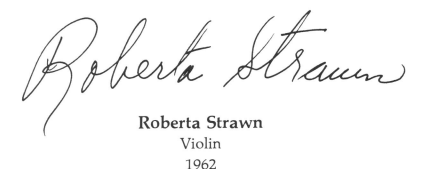

Roberta Strawn
Violin
1962

Born in Cleveland of Russian parents, **Gary Tishkoff** became interested in music when an older brother began playing the piano. When he was five, his parents bought him a violin and took him to Helen Hanon at the Cleveland Music School Settlement. Soon thereafter his family moved to the West coast, traveling by train, a mode of transport that remains an interest of his.

During his high school years in Los Angeles, he studied with Anna May Brodetsky and Joachim Chassman. He then sang with the Gregg Smith Singers and the Roger Wagner Chorale before playing with the orchestras of Utah, St. Louis, and Pittsburgh. He also toured as soloist and concertmaster of the Virginia Symphony and served as concertmaster of the Lake George Opera Festival Orchestra.

In his spare time, Mr. Tishkoff gives private lessons in his home and enjoys Chinese and Mexican cooking, as well as nature photography. He and his wife have a son, who is studying clarinet on a scholarship, and a daughter.

Eight musicians have spent their entire professional careers as members of The Cleveland Orchestra. Average tenure with the Orchestra is twenty-one years.

Gary Tishkoff
Violin
1966

Born in Chicago of Czech parents and fluent in their native language, **Richard Voldrich** attended Chicago Musical College, earning bachelor's and master's degrees in music education. He has studied with Raymond Niwa, Morris Gomberg, and John Weicher.

Before coming to Cleveland, Mr. Voldrich served as second assistant concertmaster of the St. Louis Symphony and assistant concertmaster of the St. Louis Little Symphony. He also played in Chicago's Grant Park Orchestra.

In 1982, he completed a bachelor's degree in accounting at Case Western Reserve University and passed the certified public accountant exam in 1983.

Richard Voldrich
Violin
1967

Stephen Warner, a native of Philadelphia, began to study the violin at age six. Although members of his family are musically inclined, he is the first to have made music his career. As a young student he moved with his family to Atlanta, where the Atlanta Music Club and the Georgia Power Company awarded him a three-year scholarship to the Brevard Music Center. The Atlanta Music Club also sponsored him at the University of Georgia and CIM.

At CIM he studied with David Cerone and Orchestra member Bernhard Goldschmidt, both of whom had a major influence on his work. Later Mr. Warner attended the Meadowmount School, directed by Ivan Galamian, and continued studying with Mr. Galamian on scholarship at Curtis. He also worked there with Mr. Cerone, Jascha Brodsky, Felix Galimir, and Isadore Cohen. Mr. Warner graduated from Curtis in 1979, after spending two summers on scholarship at the Blossom Festival School.

He and his wife Carolyn Gadiel Warner perform as the Cleveland Duo, a chamber music ensemble that has played throughout the U.S. The Duo's repertoire includes works for combinations of violin/piano, two violins, and violin/viola, as well as duo concerti with chamber orchestra.

Mr. Warner enjoys tours with the Orchestra, particularly since for him there is no separation from his wife. In addition, Mr. Warner relaxes by boating, camping, hiking, and traveling. At one point he considered engineering as a career, and still enjoys the mechanical aspects of many of the household, automobile, and boat repair projects he undertakes.

Stephen Warner
Violin
1979

"I started studying the violin when I was nine, because the boy next door played it," recalls **Maurice Wolfson**. Mr. Wolfson credits his parents with his early love of music, but it was not love at first sight.

Mr. Wolfson began to think of music as a career when he was in high school, and never really considered anything else. He was a scholarship student at the Boston Music School Settlement and also studied in New York. He played in the Boston Pops and San Antonio Symphony before coming to Cleveland.

Stravinsky was Mr. Wolfson's most memorable guest conductor. "It was a great thrill to have Stravinsky up on the podium, and in later years I realized that I had been in contact with a great genius."

Mr. and Mrs. Wolfson have a married daughter, Saralee Epstein, and grandaughter, Nili. Saralee is a member of the Shalhavet Dance Group at the Jewish Community Center and has performed solos at many of the Group's dance recitals.

Mrs. Wolfson has been a member of the Jewish Community Center for many years and chairs the cultural arts department volunteers. She is a recipient of the coveted Kronenberg Award for her many years of dedicated service.

Maurice Wolfson
Violin
1945

Robert Zimmer
Violin
1966

Classical music and the violin have been major forces in **Robert Zimmer's** life since he was four years old. As a teenager he began twelve years of training with Emile Bouillet, who was a strong influence on the young musician. When he was sixteen, Mr. Zimmer joined the Fort Wayne Philharmonic and later played with the Indianapolis Symphony. He formerly taught at Butler and DePauw Universities. Since 1973 he has also served as an assistant librarian for The Cleveland Orchestra.

During The Cleveland Orchestra's most recent overseas tour, Mr. Zimmer was particularly impressed by the hospitality of the American business community in Hong Kong. The Orchestra felt especially welcome there, and audiences received them with great warmth.

Mr. Zimmer has built a number of harpsichords. He particularly enjoys photography and has recently experimented with various techniques. Mr. Zimmer and his wife Betty, a pianist and teacher at CIM, frequently perform recitals together.

A Cleveland native whose first orchestral position was with the Kansas City Philharmonic, **Muriel Carmen** was one of the first women to play in The Cleveland Orchestra.

As a child, Miss Carmen listened to radio concerts and records, and at age seven began to study the violin. She received help and encouragement from her parents and devoted an enormous amount of time to practice, because she loved it. "That is the way it was with most of us who decided to become professional musicians," Miss Carmen stated. "You excelled, were encouraged, and your life went toward a musical career."

Miss Carmen recalls that Ralph Katz had a great influence on her career by providing free lessons at a time when her parents could not afford them. During her college years at Western Reserve University, she studied viola with Tom Brennand and Cleveland Orchestra member Frederick Funkhouser, and violin with Felix Eyle. While attending WRU, where she received a bachelor's degree in music education and English literature, she answered the University Orchestra's need for a violist.

She has taught both music and science in Cleveland public schools and served on the faculties of CIM and the Cleveland Music School Settlement. During that time she was active both as a recitalist and performer in many chamber music groups.

"I was teaching at the Institute when I auditioned for George Szell in 1951," she recalls. "It was only when I read the paper that I learned I had been engaged by The Cleveland Orchestra!"

For years Miss Carmen was the only professional musician in her family. However, she has been joined by her nephew Eric Carmen, formerly the lead singer with a rock group. He is now arranging and composing.

"I love Cleveland," concludes Miss Carmen. "Everything is here, the Orchestra, museums, and the Play House."

Muriel Carmen
Viola
1951

49

Yarden Faden

Viola

1966

Yarden Faden began piano lessons with his mother at age five. An accomplished professional, she soon realized the piano was not for her son. At the age of seven, however, Mr. Faden was entranced as he watched his uncle play the violin, and his parents quickly encouraged him to study that instrument.

Mr. Faden earned his bachelor of music education and master of music degrees from Northwestern University, where he was a scholarship student. Although he began his college studies with Eduardo Fiorelli on violin, he switched to the viola in his senior year. He continued viola studies through graduate school with Harold Klatz. Concurrently with his college studies, he played with the Chicago Little Symphony and appeared as soloist with the Northwestern University Orchestra under Thor Johnson, and on the television program "Artist's Showcase." Mr. Faden also studied with Abraham Skernick, former Cleveland Orchestra principal violist, at the Congress of Strings in Puerto Rico, where he was chosen to be principal violist of the Contemporary Orchestra.

After graduate school, he became a member of the Grant Park Symphony in Chicago, playing there each summer from 1962 through 1966. During three of these years, he and his wife Kirsten, a cellist, taught stringed instruments in the Atlanta public schools and played in the Atlanta Symphony. Mr. Faden was assistant principal violist of the Atlanta Symphony and was soloist in each of his three years there. He also played with the Pittsburgh Symphony for one season.

Since joining The Cleveland Orchestra, Mr. Faden has appeared as a recitalist and a member of various chamber music ensembles, including the Severance Chamber Ensemble, the Well-Tempered Players, and the Coventry Chamber Players. He has served on four Cleveland Orchestra committees, twice during contract negotiating years.

Among the interests Mr. Faden shares with his wife and two teenage children are gardening, camping, and bicycling. He has recently developed an interest in ice skating and has reached the level of intermediate second class.

Fred Funkhouser (signature)

Frederick Funkhouser
Viola
1929

When not weaving lovely melodies on his over 400-year-old viola, **Frederick Funkhouser** is weaving authentic Scottish tartan afghans on his eight-harness loom. These are the primary activities of this fifty-five-year member of The Cleveland Orchestra.

Mr. Funkhouser came to the Orchestra from Oberlin, where he graduated Phi Beta Kappa with degrees in music from the Conservatory and English from the College. He also studied in Paris under André Touret and in Czechoslovakia under Otakar Sevcik. Mr. Funkhouser's early training began at home at the age of eight where, with his mother as pianist and his brother as cellist, he made up a trio.

He planned to continue playing the violin and auditioned for that section with The Cleveland Orchestra, but there were no openings. He diligently practiced the viola for a week, had a second audition, and has never regretted the change of instrument.

Mr. Funkhouser especially appreciates the viola's lower range. His instrument, made in Cremona by Andrea Amati in 1568, is probably the oldest instrument played in an American orchestra. Its existence seems somewhat miraculous, for it was sent from Finland to Sweden before Russian bombing began in 1946. Unfortunately, all of the papers noting the instrument's owners and history were lost. Mr. Funkhouser purchased this viola by telephone.

Mr. Funkhouser counts performances with Ansermet, as well as at the Severance mansion after Mr. Severance's death, among his most special musical experiences. Orchestra tours also have been memorable. For the enthusiastic Russian audiences, Mr. Funkhouser had to wear a very hot, heavy, outsized suit because twelve trunks were lost during the tour. He also recalls the dedication of Japanese audiences; one listener had traveled eight hours by train to hear the Orchestra.

Mr. Funkhouser has taught at CIM, University School, and the University of Akron. He was named assistant principal violist in 1946.

Presently he spends his free time weaving and has made 145 double-weave afghans. There are examples of his work in Vienna, Paris, the Netherlands, West Germany, Canada, and in twenty-one states. His wife Mary also weaves.

Mr. Funkhouser has only two regrets: he wishes he had heard the premiere performance of *The Rite of Spring* and is sorry he missed seeing the first forward pass.

Lucien Joel

Lucien Joel
Viola
1969

Lucien Joel was born in Antwerp, Belgium, and began studying the violin at the age of five with his father. In high school he switched to the viola. Gerard Ruymen was his mentor at the Royal Conservatory of Music in Antwerp, from which Mr. Joel received the solo diploma and government gold medal. Upon graduation, he took a position as second principal viola with the Het Brabants Orkest, Netherlands. He continued to study in Antwerp with Mr. Ruymen until he came to Cleveland.

Mr. Joel plays a most unusual viola; there are only five like it in the world. The viola was made in 1964 at the Mittenwald School for Violin Builders. The director of the school used an exceptional combination of very new and very old techniques in its construction. It was put together electronically and then varnished and dried naturally as instruments were 100 years ago. Most conventional violas need to be broken in for a year or so, but this one produced such a fine tone that it was used in a solo concert only one week after it was completed.

Mr. Joel, his wife Carol, and their two children enjoy hiking in Cleveland's Metropolitan Parks. Both children play the violin and piano. Mr. Joel plays chamber music with the Cleveland State University Trio.

Mr. Joel currently teaches viola at Cleveland State University and CIM. He feels that children should begin studying music when they exhibit the desire to learn, have a sense of rhythm, and are willing to practice and work hard.

Born in Chicago of Hungarian parents, **William Kiraly** at age four showed an interest in and fascination for music, listening to Vienna Philharmonic recordings of Strauss waltzes. He first studied violin at age eleven and volunteered to change to the viola in high school.

He earned his bachelor's degree from CIM and received a master's in music history from Western Reserve University. Mr. Kiraly's teachers were Tom Brennand, Marcel Dick, and Cleveland Orchestra member Frederick Funkhouser.

Mr. Kiraly was principal violist of the Kansas City Philharmonic and Independence, Missouri Orchestra. Currently he is a member of the Well-Tempered Players. His viola was made by Tonini in 1683. Mr. Kiraly plays the Baroque violin and viola da gamba as well.

The author of articles for *Northern Ohio Live, The Christian Science Monitor, Piano Quarterly, American Organist, Musical America, Diapason,* and The Cleveland Orchestra program book, Mr. Kiraly also has written jointly with his wife Philippa for many journals.

He especially enjoyed the Orchestra's 1979 tour of Europe, which included Budapest, where he was able to find the private school he attended as a teenager.

Mr. Kiraly's special interest is early music, with particular emphasis on the historical accuracy of its performance. He enjoys listening to compositions by Mozart, Monteverdi, Gibbons, Byrd, and Marenzio. With his wife, he created a harpsichord from a puzzle of 3,000 pieces. They worked nearly day and night for over three months to complete the instrument.

William Kiraly
Viola
1947

A native of Cicero, Illinois, **Arthur Klima** began to study violin at the age of six to please his parents. One year later he was playing in the school orchestra. By the time he was in high school, Mr. Klima was quite serious about music; so much so that he gave up a first-string position on the basketball team in order to remain in the orchestra. He recalls that "by the end of high school I knew I was setting my sights on one of the big five orchestras."

With a friend's encouragement Mr. Klima first tried a viola in high school. Immediately enjoying the sound of the instrument, he began to teach himself to play it. This auspicious start led to bachelor's and master's degrees from the University of Illinois and Yale University, respectively. John Garvey, Paul Rolland, Harold Klatz, and Walter Trampler were among his viola instructors.

Mr. Klima spent the first four years of his professional career with the Baltimore Symphony before joining The Cleveland Orchestra. During his tenure in Cleveland, he has performed in chamber music concerts and taught at Baldwin-Wallace College from 1978 to 1982.

In addition to arranging viola transcriptions of various cello works and voraciously reading seventeenth-, eighteenth-, and nineteenth-century novels, Mr. Klima enjoys his collection of succulent plants.

Arthur Klima
Viola
1977

While most Orchestra members realized their desire to become musicians at an early age, twelve percent pursued formal training in areas such as English literature, urban affairs, accounting, medicine, journalism, and psychology.

Vitold Kushleika

Vitold Kushleika
Viola
1944

Vitold Kushleika says that American audiences are a pleasure, but the acclaim and wild enthusiasm The Cleveland Orchestra enjoys in the major European music centers is something he will never forget. He also marvels at some Japanese parents, who carefully save up to fifty dollars for each ticket so that their children can hear the Orchestra.

Mr. Kushleika finds great pleasure in performing chamber music and solo recitals for churches and charitable organizations. Mr. Kushleika's two children happen to be musical, and he believes that all can enrich their lives by exposure to fine music.

As a child in Bridgewater, Massachusetts, Mr. Kushleika studied the violin and piano. Later he found he had a natural aptitude for the viola: "I liked the viola's dark sound and I was physically large enough to handle it easily." Mr. Kushleika's interest in music also is manifest in his collection of violins and bows, which places an emphasis on modern Italian instruments. He enjoys studying the theory of tone production as it relates to violin making and seeks out violin makers and collectors in his travels. He is considered to be very knowledgeable about the quality of certain string instruments.

After scholarship studies at Tanglewood and Eastman, where he received a performer's certificate and bachelor of music degree, he subsequently earned a master of arts degree from Case Western Reserve University. Before coming to The Cleveland Orchestra, Mr. Kushleika played with the Houston Symphony, the Rochester Philharmonic, and the Pittsburgh Symphony.

Music was a natural part of the environment in **Edward Ormond's** childhood home. His older brother and sister played the piano, and his father, who worked on the first phonographs with Thomas Edison, brought one of the early machines home along with many records to be played.

Mr. Ormond began playing the piano at an early age but begged for a violin after attending a violin recital with his father. He later commuted between his home in Newark, New Jersey, and New York to study with Samuel Gardner. While he attended the University of Michigan, where he earned his bachelor of music degree in violin, he enjoyed playing the viola and often volunteered to play it when needed. During World War II, while stationed in England, he was a frequent violin soloist but joined an army string quartet as a violist. (He met his wife while in England.) After the war he returned to the University of Michigan and made the final switch when a teacher observed that he was playing the violin like a violist, and proceeded to earn his M.M. in viola.

He was assistant principal violist of both the Indianapolis and St. Louis Symphonies before becoming the first assistant principal violist of The Cleveland Orchestra. Mr. Ormond has been very active in many chamber groups and is currently a member of the Cleveland Octet. He has played in the Casals Festival for many years and is a member of the faculty of CIM.

"The Szell days were filled with memorable musical experiences," said Mr. Ormond. Mr. Szell was "all business, devotion, and musical insight," and Mr. Ormond most appreciated the quality of playing he extracted from each Orchestra member.

Other highlights of his career include the Orchestra's four tours of the Far East, as well as their visit to the Soviet Union. One outstanding memory involves his visit with Mr. Suzuki at his school. They discussed his famous method of instruction and listened to many of his students.

Mr. Ormond plays a very special Amati viola, dated 1619. It was loaned to him by an architect and amateur violist in St. Louis. Upon the architect's death, Mr. Ormond was given the first opportunity to buy the instrument.

Mr. Ormond and his wife Mimi, who recently retired from a position as a nursery school director, have three daughters: one is a professional artist, one is the piccolo (and flute) player with the Milwaukee Symphony, and one is a freelance violist in Chicago. They also have a grandson, who plays a pint-sized violin.

Edward Ormond
Viola
1959

There have been two major upheavals in **Walter Stummer's** life. The first occurred in 1945 when, at the age of twenty, he and his family left Czechoslovakia for Austria after their estate was lost to the Communists. The second was his immigration to the United States five years later. In both instances, music enabled Mr. Stummer to make his way and build a new life in a foreign country.

After settling in Austria, Mr. Stummer entered the Mozarteum in Salzburg. His parents encouraged him "to turn what was music for pleasure into music as a profession." He recalls growing up with music being "a part of our environment, a normal part of our home life like TV is today." Mr. Stummer's aunt, a concert pianist, lived with his family, and both his father and grandmother sang and played the piano. Mr. Stummer was taught piano by his grandmother, and near the age of six he began to play the violin. He was self-taught on the violin as a child, except for occasional lessons during visits to Vienna with his family.

At the age of twenty-two, while studying in Salzburg with Christa Richter-Steiner, Mr. Stummer began to play the viola. He notes that he was "a little heavy-handed for the violin, but I was a natural for the viola; the viola immediately sounded better than the violin." Mr. Stummer met his wife Barbara while they were fellow students at the Mozarteum, where she was studying piano.

After arriving in the U.S., Mr. Stummer decided to pursue a career as a professional musician. He spent his days working in the darkroom of a photo shop, and he "practiced like mad" on the viola and violin from 8:00 to 11:00 P.M. at the social hall of his parish church. His efforts were not in vain. In 1952 he was appointed to the Indianapolis Symphony and came to Cleveland one year later.

Recently Mr. Stummer has ventured into composition. He has completed a suite in four movements for viola and is currently working on the second movement of another work. Mr. Stummer has derived a great deal of satisfaction from composing and hopes to perform his suite publicly. He has been strongly influenced by Hindemith and recalls a young conductor who, in helping him work through a Hindemith sonata, opened his mind to modern symphonic music.

Mr. Stummer is also talented in working with wood. He has created sculptures as well as functional pieces such as furniture and bowls. Other interests include gardening, poetry, and composing limericks.

Walter Stummer
Viola
1953

Ursula Urbaniak Sicre's musical studies commenced at the age of four with piano lessons, which she continued until junior high school. At that time she opted to study the cello but, because of parental encouragement, ultimately selected the violin.

In high school she studied violin with Nathan Gottschalk, who provided considerable guidance and encouragement. After graduation Ms. Urbaniak Sicre attended Hartt College of Music of the University of Hartford in Connecticut. Her teachers included Raphael Bronstein and Arianna Bronne.

She studied with Raphael Druian at the Second International String Congress and has played chamber music at Tanglewood with Joseph Silverstein and William Kroll. In 1967 Ms. Urbaniak Sicre toured Europe and the United States with the Accademia Musicale Napolitana Chamber Orchestra.

Ms. Urbaniak Sicre became an accomplished violist while she was with the Hartford Symphony and eventually became principal there. She then served as assistant principal of the Dallas Symphony for two years. A native of Hartford, she enjoys returning home to perform during The Cleveland Orchestra's East Coast tours. She also teaches at the Summer Music Experience in Hudson.

Music has played a significant role in Ms. Urbaniak Sicre's life. She feels exposure to music is important for everyone, especially young people. Her four children are growing up in a musical home, studying various instruments and attending Orchestra concerts. She is married to Orchestra cellist Jorge Sicre.

Ursula Urbaniak Sicre
Viola
1981

"I started playing the violin at nine," recalls Canadian-born **Robert Vernon**, "and knew then I wanted to become a musician." Without telling his parents of his plans, Mr. Vernon showed them by his dedication. "I got up at 5:30 every morning to practice. I was very disciplined because I knew what I wanted. Initially my parents were very encouraging. At a certain point however, my father, a Presbyterian minister, felt musicians were like actors; unless you were really good, you would starve."

Mr. Vernon received the Martha Dwight Douglas Foundation Scholarship to Juilliard and graduated with honors. His teachers were Ivan Galamian and Sally Thomas. Before coming to Cleveland as principal violist, he was associate principal of the St. Louis Symphony.

Mr. Vernon has performed at a number of major music festivals, including the Marlboro and Aspen Festivals, and was elected a corporate member of the Music Associates of Aspen. Moreover, he recently was appointed to the faculty of the New College Music Festival in Sarasota, Florida. He has collaborated in chamber music with such artists as Lorin Maazel, Rudolf Serkin, Lynn Harrell, Elmar Oliveira, Shlomo Mintz, Lee Luvisi, and the late William Primrose. He has given numerous highly acclaimed recitals throughout the country.

Mr. Vernon is a member of the Cleveland Orchestra String Quartet and participated in Telarc's digital recording of Chausson's Concerto for Piano, Violin, and String Quartet, op. 21, with Lorin Maazel and Israela Margalit. He also has recorded as soloist with the Orchestra on the London label.

Mr. Vernon is chairman of the viola department at CIM and serves on the faculty of the Blossom Festival School. He also has taught at the Cleveland Chamber Music Seminar and frequently teaches master classes at universities.

As a soloist Mr. Vernon has been enthusiastically received across the U.S. He has appeared in that role with The Cleveland Orchestra in Severance Hall, Carnegie Hall, and Boston's Symphony Hall. In 1981 he soloed with the Orchestra in Lincoln Center's Great Performers Series. Mr. Vernon has recently appeared with the St. Louis Symphony, Chicago's Grant Park Symphony, Denver Symphony, Aspen Chamber Orchestra, Sarasota Festival Orchestra, Omaha Symphony, and Florida West Coast Symphony.

Mr. Vernon manages to fit an occasional game of golf into his busy schedule. His wife Valerie is a violist as well.

Robert Vernon
Viola
1976

As a freshman at CIM **Ralph Curry** walked past Severance Hall with a fellow student and announced, "In five years, I am going to be here." His prediction proved correct; he joined the Orchestra just before his twenty-third birthday. Mr. Curry's entire career has been goal-directed; he knew from age twelve he would become a professional musician. Music was a predominant force in the Curry home. His brother William Henry Curry is now assistant conductor of the Indianapolis and St. Paul Symphony Orchestras. Although he describes his musical career as a series of "lucky choices," in the end he believes that "music chooses you, you don't choose it."

The recent appearances of Colin Davis with The Cleveland Orchestra were very special for Mr. Curry. He considers Sir Colin to be a conductor of the finest caliber and a very warm human being.

Mr. Curry's first tour with the Orchestra, the 1978 Far East tour, was his most exciting, despite the culture shock he experienced. He remembers in particular the traffic jams in Tokyo, when it took Orchestra members one and a half hours to ride the four-mile trip by bus to and from rehearsals and then again to performances. He enjoys experiencing new audiences and found the South American audiences "unbelievably enthusiastic . . . wall to wall people, wanting more and more encores."

Mr. Curry teaches at Cleveland State University. His teaching philosophy is that "students should understand that becoming a professional musician requires working incredibly hard, setting long-term goals, and making the right choices based on those goals." He is also a member of a new chamber music group, The Severance Trio, with Vladimir and Lyubov Deninzon. He has participated in a faculty trio at Cleveland State University with Orchestra members Eric Eichhorn and Lucien Joel as well. When not involved in musical activities, Mr. Curry enjoys his newly discovered love, tennis.

Ralph Curry
Cello
1978

Stephen Geber comes from a family of cellists. His father Edwin recently retired as cellist with the Los Angeles Philharmonic but continues to teach cello. His mother Gretchen teaches cello and has done extensive chamber and studio work. His brother is a cellist with the American String Quartet.

Mr. Geber began to study the piano at the age of six. However, he really wanted to play the cello, so his mother began to teach him when he was eight years old. Subsequent teachers were Gabor Rejto and Stephen Deák. Throughout his youth, a keen interest in baseball and track competed with Mr. Geber's musical studies. He attended Eastman on full scholarship and earned a bachelor of music degree with honors in 1965 and a performer's certificate. While there, he studied with Ronald Leonard and played with the Rochester Philharmonic and Eastman-Rochester Symphony. He later worked with Zara Nelsova.

Before he joined The Cleveland Orchestra as principal cellist, Mr. Geber played with the Boston Symphony and taught at the New England Conservatory of Music. Presently he teaches cello, chamber music, and orchestral repertoire at CIM. In addition, he teaches at the Blossom Festival School, gives tour master classes, and plays with the Cleveland Orchestra String Quartet.

He has appeared as soloist with the Rochester Philharmonic, Boston Pops Orchestra, and on many occasions with The Cleveland Orchestra, both in Cleveland and on tour, including two appearances in Carnegie Hall. Mr. Geber has also done extensive chamber and recital work throughout the country.

Mr. Geber feels that a deep love of music is essential for one to succeed as a professional musician. He very much admires Mstislav Rostropovich and Lynn Harrell and describes the music of Mahler as "emotionally hair-raising."

He is married to Lisa Wellbaum, The Cleveland Orchestra's principal harpist. They have a three-year-old daughter, Stephanie, "who has great rhythm and pitch for her age," and an infant daughter Lauren. Mr. Geber has two older daughters, Pamela and Kristin, of whom he is very proud. They are active in modern dance, ballet, and piano.

In his free time, Mr. Geber enjoys reading about current events and studying history. He maintains an active interest in sports and listens to classical music, jazz, James Galway, and Chuck Mangione, who was a classmate of his at Eastman. He loves Cleveland for its wonderful residential areas and wealth of cultural institutions and activities.

Stephen Geber
Cello
1973

Music was an integral part of the environment in **Thomas Mansbacher's** home. His parents played the piano, and his sister played the violin. He began playing cello in the fourth grade, and by the age of thirteen was a soloist with the University City Orchestra in St. Louis.

"We had a game—musical detective—we often played at the dinner table. We listened to the radio or records, and tried to guess the piece of music, the composer or his nationality or century, or some other detail. My mother knew all the answers," he recalls.

Mr. Mansbacher considered music to be only an avocation until he graduated from college. He earned a degree in urban affairs from Washington University, but supported himself with his music from the age of eighteen. He played with the St. Louis Little Symphony, the Concordia Seminary Kantorei, and the St. Louis Municipal Opera, where he was principal cellist for many years.

However, when he decided to attend graduate school music was his major, and he received an M.M. from the Yale School of Music. Mr. Mansbacher was principal cellist of the Symphonies of New Haven, Springfield, and New Hampshire. He also played with the Boston Ballet and the Opera Company of Boston. He studied quartet technique with the Yale and Guarnieri Quartets, and his teachers were George Neikrug, Aldo Parisot, and Elizabeth K. Fischer.

He particularly enjoys chamber music and recalls with satisfaction his performance of the three Bach gamba sonatas with harpsichord. Mr. Mansbacher also is committed to contemporary music and is a member of Reconnaissance.

Since his youth, Mr. Mansbacher has enjoyed practicing. He still practices three or four consecutive hours, although this sometimes proves impractical when he is with his two young daughters. Along with his wife Sallie, he is an avid reader, does not own a television, loves sushi, and is a fan of Woody Allen and Alfred Hitchcock. He particularly enjoyed the Orchestra's tours to Japan for that country's cultural and culinary pleasures.

Mr. Mansbacher believes that The Cleveland Orchestra contributes significantly to the quality of life in Cleveland, and that the city respects its orchestra. "Blossom concerts are the best thing about summers in Cleveland," he commented.

Thomas Mansbacher
Cello
1977

Deeply felt convictions regarding peace and human understanding permeate **Diane Mather's** personal and professional life, from her motivating role in the successful Musicians Against Nuclear Arms concert in 1982, to her warm stories of experiences with people encountered during the Orchestra's foreign tours. She enjoys the small-town nature of Cleveland that fosters both a closeness among Orchestra members and familiarity with concertgoers.

Music has been an integral part of Miss Mather's experience for longer than she can remember. Her mother, who was her first teacher, and her father were professional pianists and organists, and her sister plays the violin. She chose the cello as her instrument after hearing her mother repeatedly bemoan the lack of good cellists for trios. Family trio performances became common as the girls grew up.

Despite this strong musical background, early adolescent shyness drove Miss Mather's talents underground until her high school orchestra director and two orchestra members persuaded her not to conceal her abilities. Then Leonard Rose, whom she met at summer music camp, encouraged her to study at Curtis rather than follow the family's Ivy League footsteps. She enjoyed continued success at Curtis despite a broken back, which put her in a body cast for one year, making cello transport and playing enormously difficult.

Mr. Rose again influenced Miss Mather's career choice in 1963 when she completed her studies at Curtis. He strongly urged her to audition for George Szell and The Cleveland Orchestra. She joined the Orchestra that year and was appointed assistant principal cellist in 1967. She received her M.M. from CIM and has studied with Orlando Cole and Ernst Silberstein, as well as Leonard Rose. She also plays with the Cuyahoga Valley Arts Ensemble and has appeared as a soloist with the Hartford Symphony, The Cleveland Orchestra, the Suburban Symphony, and the Cleveland Women's Orchestra.

Diane Mather and her husband William Klima have two children, Molly and Samuel.

Diane Mather

Cello

1963

Catharina Meints considers herself an "evangelist" in spreading an interest in Baroque music. Ms. Meints teaches at the Baroque Performance Institute, a school she and her husband James Caldwell organized at Oberlin College, which draws students from all over the country each summer. She considers her teaching at the Institute an extremely satisfying and creative outlet. She also is a virtuoso on the viola da gamba and studied the instrument in Basel, Switzerland, with August Wenzinger. In addition to teaching at the Institute and Oberlin, she plays with the Oberlin Baroque Ensemble and Cleveland Baroque Soloists.

Ms. Meints began playing piano at four, violin with her mother as teacher at six, and cello at eight. Five summers of study at Interlochen as a teenager pointed her toward a future in music. She earned a bachelor's degree and performer's certificate at Eastman. She credits her husband, a professor of oboe at Oberlin, with introducing her to the viola da gamba and her subsequent love of Baroque music.

Ms. Meints' interest in Baroque music extends to period instruments. She and her husband have a personal collection of eighty Baroque string instruments, mostly violas da gamba. The cello she plays with the Orchestra was crafted in 1796.

Before joining The Cleveland Orchestra, she played with the Chamber Symphony of Philadelphia, the Rochester Philharmonic, and the National Symphony. She has performed gamba solos with The Cleveland Orchestra and the Smithsonian Chamber Players, and cello solos with the North Olmsted Orchestra.

Ms. Meints has thoroughly enjoyed the change in her life since the arrival of her two-year-old son Jonathan.

Catharina Meints
Cello
1971

Robert Perry
Cello
1968

Musical studies for **Robert Perry** began early in grade school where he learned to read music well enough to sing in his church children's choir. Since he always had liked string instruments, he took the opportunity to study cello in the seventh grade, when anyone willing to try was offered an instrument and free lessons. Mr. Perry recalls, "My father, a French horn player and always interested in my musical studies, was very helpful."

Mr. Perry received his music degrees from Ithaca College and the University of Illinois. He has studied cello with Forrest Sanders, Peter Farrell, and Claus Adam.

During his military service, when he was obliged to live without music, it became clear to Mr. Perry that music must become a permanent part of his life. He subsequently held positions as assistant professor of music at the Universities of Kentucky and Nevada, and as associate professor at Ithaca College.

While on a sabbatical leave, he found himself playing in the Chamber Symphony of Philadelphia. That experience proved to him that playing in a good orchestra "seemed to feel just right." He has also played in the Ithaca String Quartet and the Aspen Festival and Casals Festival Orchestras.

George Szell embodied the characteristics Mr. Perry believes make a great conductor: the obvious artistry and rehearsal techniques plus a serious, dedicated, and humble approach to the preparation and performance of music. "A great conductor is a voice through which music is heard," he observes.

Mr. Perry finds many things about the Cleveland area appealing: boating on Lake Erie, the museums, and the artistic community. He is an accomplished painter, has built his own sailboat, and enjoys gardening and woodworking.

His wife Alcestis is a well-known area violinist. They have two children, a son and a daughter.

Jorge Sicre
Cello
1961

Born in Havana of parents very supportive of his musical pursuits, **Jorge Sicre** first began to study cello at age seven. Mr. Sicre always has been fascinated and thrilled by string instruments and needed little inducement to practice. His father bought his first cello from a pawnshop for twenty-eight pesos. Mr. Sicre now owns one made in Milan by Carlo Guiseppe Testore in 1690.

He received most of his music education at Juilliard. Mr. Sicre's principal teacher, Leonard Rose, was most helpful in enriching and expanding his musical perspectives. Thanks to his previous teacher, Oswaldo Mazzucchi of the NBC Symphony, he was able to listen in on Toscanini's rehearsals, which was quite a privilege and thrill for a sixteen-year-old. Later Mr. Sicre studied in Paris with Paul Tortelier.

After graduating from Juilliard, he formed the Alard Quartet, which still has one original member and is now quartet-in-residence at the University of Pennsylvania. He played with the Severance String Quartet for four years and now coaches chamber music at the Blossom Festival School.

Mr. Sicre was principal cellist of the Havana Philharmonic and performed solos in Cuba and Miami. He particularly enjoys performing chamber music and the works of Mozart, Beethoven, Shostakovich, and Prokofiev. He has fond memories of working with George Szell.

Mr. Sicre appreciates Cleveland's changing seasons, Art Museum, and the resident acting company at the Play House. He plans to publish a book of caricatures of famous musicians (having perhaps inherited his artistic talent from his sculptor father). His son Jorge Luis is a gifted painter who has exhibited in Cleveland, New York, and Philadelphia. Mr. Sicre is married to Orchestra violist Ursula Urbaniak Sicre.

Martin Simon came to the United States from Germany by way of Italy and France before World War II. He served in the armed forces and subsequently joined The Cleveland Orchestra. While performing with the Orchestra, Mr. Simon attended CIM and received his bachelor's and master's degrees in music. He also studied musicology. Mr. Simon cites as particularly meaningful and motivating the time he spent studying with Ernst Silberstein, Luigi Silva, and Pierre Fournier.

Mr. Simon has performed with the Houston and the Pittsburgh Symphonies, and has appeared as soloist with the Cleveland Women's Orchestra. He particularly enjoys chamber music and for ten years was the leader of a string quartet that performed for children in the schools under the auspices of the Music Performance Trust Fund.

Mr. Simon taught cello for fourteen years at the Phillis Wheatley Association and now teaches privately. Mr. Simon's cello is a Francesco Ruggeri Dett 'Il Per made in Cremona, Italy, in 1679.

When he is not performing with the Orchestra, Mr. Simon is busy studying psychology and the French language. He has a knowledge of German and Italian as well. Of special interest to Mr. Simon are nuclear arms education (through Physicians for Social Responsibility), the Nuclear Weapons Freeze Campaign, and the Linus Pauling Institute.

Mr. Simon has two daughters, one of whom has studied the sitar in India.

Martin Simon
Cello
1947

Gary Stucka
Cello
1981

Gary Stucka began playing the cello at the age of eight, receiving much support and encouragement from his mother, an accomplished pianist, and a family of enthusiastic music lovers. At age seventeen he had the opportunity to participate in the Tanglewood program as an orchestral musician, and this experience was decisive in his choice of career. He developed a very special feeling for orchestral music which has remained with him ever after.

Mr. Stucka received his bachelor's and master's degrees in cello performance from the Chicago Musical College of Roosevelt University. Mr. Stucka feels that Karl Fruh at the Chicago Music College was an influential and constructive teacher because he allowed Mr. Stucka to develop his own form of expression on the cello rather than "imitate the master."

After graduation he served as principal cellist of the Winnipeg Symphony and as assistant principal of Chicago's Grant Park Symphony. Mr. Stucka was soloist on four occasions with the Winnipeg Symphony and also with several orchestras in Chicago.

He came to Cleveland in 1981, enticed here by the high standards and integrity of Cleveland Orchestra musicians. He enjoys The Cleveland Orchestra very much and feels keenly that "there is a chemistry here which is created by the players. They listen to each other and in doing so form a tightness in performance."

Mr. Stucka is a member of the Cleveland Octet. In addition to many other interests, he enjoys collecting rare instrumental and orchestral 78 r.p.m. phonograph records. He owns several antique phonographs, two of which play Edison cylinders.

Richard Weiss

Cello

1974

A native of Los Angeles, **Richard Weiss** began his study of the cello at age ten. His first few years of playing coincided with a keen interest in the martial art of judo. Although the word "judo" means "the gentle way," he found it was not a gentle enough activity for an increasingly serious cello student who needed to keep all his fingers unbroken.

While in high school Mr. Weiss was chosen to represent California in the Music Teachers National Association competition and was national first prize winner of the string player division. At the Tanglewood Festival he was principal cellist and winner of the Young Artist Program concerto contest, earning the solo spot for the Festival's culminating concert.

Mr. Weiss was awarded a full merit scholarship to attend Eastman, where he served as principal cellist of the Eastman Philharmonia and played professionally in the Rochester Philharmonic. He was in summer residence at Harvard University as a member of the Harvard Chamber Players.

Halfway through his work at Eastman, Mr. Weiss received a most frightening and valuable lesson. Thinking of transferring to Juilliard, he went to New York City for an audition. Walking with his cello the night before his morning appointment, he was robbed at knifepoint. Luckily, the thieves were interested more in his wallet than the "big guitar case." Mr. Weiss found that along with the loss of his cash, he had been drained of any fears that might have hindered the audition, which went very successfully. Nevertheless, he opted to finish his studies at Eastman. In retrospect, he is grateful to those thieves. Had he enrolled at Juilliard, he would have missed an important opportunity. Immediately upon being graduated from Eastman the next year, Mr. Weiss joined The Cleveland Orchestra.

Mr. Weiss was appointed first assistant principal cellist in 1978. In his debut as soloist with the Orchestra, he performed the Lalo Cello Concerto. He played the Saint-Saens Concerto with the Cleveland Sinfonia at a benefit concert for CIM. At Blossom Music Center he was featured in solo roles with the visiting ballet companies of Houston and San Francisco. Mr. Weiss has also appeared with the Orchestra in three performances of Tchaikovsky's "Variations on a Rococo Theme."

He is married to principal Orchestra keyboardist Joela Jones. Mr. Weiss has collaborated with Miss Jones and Concertmaster Daniel Majeske in a recording for the Chamber Recording label.

"Getting hit with music is like getting hit with religion," believes **Donald White**, who discovered his love for music as a teenager. Mr. White began playing the cello late in life, at the age of seventeen, when his sister became disenchanted with the instrument. Previously Mr. White had played bass tuba.

After high school Mr. White was drafted into the Navy, where he played in the Navy Band. Later he earned degrees from Roosevelt College in Chicago and the Hartt College of Music in Hartford, Connecticut. Before coming to Cleveland, he was assistant principal cellist of the Hartford Symphony and a member of a string quartet at the University of Hartford.

A faculty member at the Cleveland Music School Settlement, Mr. White feels that practicing for a musician is like training for an athlete: "you're never too good or too old to practice."

Mr. White's family is very musical. His wife Dolores teaches music and piano at Cuyahoga Community College. Their son Darrell is a violinist and scholarship student at Boston University. Their daughter studies piano and music education at Oberlin. In his spare time, Mr. White enjoys listening to WCLV or WKSU, reading, and doing crossword puzzles.

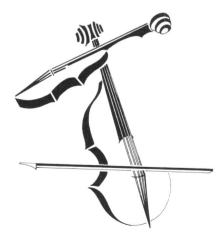

Donald White
Cello
1957

When his sixth grade class was tested for musical talent, **Harvey Wolfe** was absent. The following fall those who scored well were scheduled for the free music lessons provided by the Cleveland public schools. Though his name was not on the list, Mr. Wolfe asked to join the group, determined to learn to play the violin. However, all the violins were taken and he was handed a cello.

After a year of string classes, he enrolled at the Cleveland Music School Settlement. He also attended Cleveland Orchestra children's concerts, and spent weekends listening to records at the Cleveland Public Library. Finally his teacher, former Orchestra cellist Robert Ripley, telephoned Mr. Wolfe's mother to announce, "Your son is a musician." Convinced, his mother bought a cello for him, instead of a winter coat for herself.

Mr. Wolfe played in the Glenville High School orchestra, which had been one of the country's finest school orchestras. After graduation he studied at Tanglewood and then enrolled at CIM. In the middle of his third year there, Leopold Stokowski offered him a position with the Houston Symphony Orchestra. He played there four years, with the National Symphony for two years, and spent his summers at Aspen, Meadowmount, and CIM. He was principal of the Nashville Symphony Orchestra and Phoenix Symphony, and received his master of music degree from Arizona State University.

Though much of his time is taken up with Orchestra rehearsals, performances, and teaching at CIM, Mr. Wolfe believes that nothing can equal the depth of musical knowledge that comes from playing chamber music. He was a member of the Nashville String Quartet, which played over 500 educational concerts, and performed and taught chamber music at George Peabody College, the Taos School of Music, Wooster College, and Arizona State University. He studied with the Juilliard Quartet, Claus Adam, Leonard Rose, Zara Nelsova, and Ernst Silberstein. He is a founding member of the Coventry Chamber Players.

Mr. Wolfe is a "home town booster" who finds in Cleveland just the right combination of geographical accessibility and cultural diversity. He knows his own career would not have been possible without the commitment of Cleveland's civic resources to music and education and feels government and arts organizations must reach out to young people to counteract a too-accessible popular culture.

Mr. Wolfe, his wife Suzy, and daughters Alexandra and Stephanie live in Cleveland Heights.

Harvey Wolfe
Cello
1967

Lawrence Angell came to The Cleveland Orchestra directly following his student days at Eastman, when he was appointed to the bass section by George Szell. His promotions to assistant principal and principal followed in 1961 and 1981, respectively.

While at Eastman Mr. Angell studied bass with the very well-known Oscar Zimmerman and earned both bachelor and master of music degrees. At the same time he played several seasons with the Rochester Philharmonic under Erich Leinsdorf.

Mr. Angell has been a frequent performer of solo and chamber music for the bass. He is a member of the Scotia Chamber Players, playing and teaching in Halifax, Nova Scotia, each June.

Teaching is another strong interest, and he is head of the double bass departments of both CIM and Oberlin. His students are members of orchestras ranging from the Los Angeles Philharmonic to the Metropolitan Opera Orchestra. Mr. Angell began his own musical studies on the violin in his native Michigan; his mother was a pianist.

Two of Mr. Angell's compelling interests are tennis and airplanes; indeed, he has become an F.A.A. certified flight instructor.

Photo by Daniel Elghanayan

While the average age of Orchestra members is forty-six, the youngest member was born in 1959, and the oldest in 1905.

Lawrence Angell
Bass
1955

Mark Atherton started playing the bass in fourth grade. Both of his parents are involved in music and were supportive of his musical education, although his true motivation came from his own desire to play the bass. Mr. Atherton grew up in Schenectady, New York, and during high school he studied bass privately with David Cobb of the Albany Symphony. He was also co-captain of his high school football team. These two activities created an occasional conflict, however, as when a minor football injury prevented Mr. Atherton from performing with the Schenectady Symphony.

He attended Penn State one year as a liberal arts major, but his interest in the bass took precedence. He transferred to Boston University School for the Arts, where he graduated magna cum laude with a bachelor's degree in music. Mr. Atherton feels fortunate to have studied under Henry Portnoi, former principal bassist of the Boston Symphony Orchestra.

During college he often performed with various local groups, including the Opera Company of Boston, the Harvard Chamber Orchestra, the Boston Pops Esplanade Orchestra, and as a substitute with the Boston Symphony Orchestra. Before coming to Cleveland, he was a member of the Indianapolis Symphony for two years. While there he also taught bass at Indiana State University.

Mr. Atherton's wife Linda is a professional cellist and is involved mainly in chamber music. The Athertons share interests in the performing arts and outdoor recreation. He also enjoys playing soccer, tennis, golf, and racquetball, sports that pose a less serious threat to his career than football.

Mark Atherton
Bass
1983

Harry Barnoff came to bass playing quite by accident. His first instrument was the Hawaiian guitar, somewhat unusual for a Cleveland native. However, a junior high school teacher suggested he play the bass, "since my hands were right for it, and the school orchestra needed one."

Mr. Barnoff was a scholarship student of Hyman Goldin, Michael Lamagna, and Cleveland Orchestra member Jacques Posell at CIM, as well as Frederic Zimmerman at Juilliard. Before returning to Cleveland as an Orchestra member, he played with the U.S. Army Ground Forces Band, Youngstown Symphony, Erie Symphony Orchestra, and New York City Opera Orchestra.

He has devoted much time to teaching. Formerly on the CIM faculty, he now heads the bass departments at Cleveland State University and the Cleveland Music School Settlement. He also has been a consultant teacher for the Cleveland Board of Education for many years.

Mr. Barnoff is a frequent performer with chamber music ensembles throughout the eastern United States and has conducted many bass symposiums in Ohio, Pennsylvania, and Michigan.

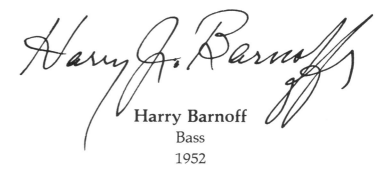

Harry Barnoff
Bass
1952

Becoming a double bass player in a major symphony orchestra was the most natural choice of profession for **Martin Flowerman.** He grew up in Brooklyn, New York, hearing the deep resonant sound of the instrument, as his father is principal bassist of the New York City Ballet Orchestra. Mr. Flowerman began studying with his father at age twelve and, after attending Juilliard, played with the American Symphony and Detroit Symphony Orchestra. At the age of twenty, the "most significant experience of my career occurred; I was selected by George Szell to join The Cleveland Orchestra."

Mr. Flowerman's most recent achievement is the publication of *Music for Double Bass Quartet.* He has arranged and transcribed music of the Renaissance and Baroque periods from several other instruments to add to literature for bass players. Mr. Flowerman performs in chamber music groups, teaches bass privately, and has coached various chamber music ensembles.

He owns two basses: one is an Italian double bass made by J. B. Lolio in 1759, and the other one is a newer instrument, 175 years old, made in Germany.

The father of two piano students, Sharon and Chad, Mr. Flowerman enjoys many aspects of life in Cleveland. Among his many hobbies, in addition to travel, are bicycling, bowling, reading, and visiting art museums. He is also a collector of records, tools, and bass figurines. He hopes someday to study psychology and philosophy and pursue his interest in writing.

Martin Flowerman
Bass
1967

Were it not for a throat problem that troubled him while playing trumpet in a jazz group, **Scott Haigh** might never have begun his career as a double bass player. His desire to continue to play in the jazz group led Mr. Haigh, at the age of fourteen, to the double bass. Jazz was not his only introduction to music, however. His father is an amateur pianist, and at eight years of age Mr. Haigh began to study piano while living in Chicago. At age fourteen he performed Mozart's Piano Concerto No. 17 with an orchestra.

At the Congress of Strings, while studying with Warren Benfield, Mr. Haigh decided to attend Northwestern University's School of Music. Two summers at the Aspen Music Festival, and study with Harold Siegel, Ring Warner, and Joseph Guastafeste all contributed to his career as a professional musician. In 1975 he joined the Orquesta Sinfonica del Estado de Mexico and then played with the Milwaukee Symphony Orchestra before coming to Cleveland.

As first assistant principal bass of The Cleveland Orchestra, Mr. Haigh fondly remembers performances of Strauss' *Ein Heldenleben* with Lorin Maazel in New York City and Brahms' Symphony No. 3 with Colin Davis in Cleveland. He also enjoys chamber music and is the solo bass player in the Cleveland Octet. He is an adjunct professor of double bass at the University of Akron and teaches privately as well.

Performing in the Teatro Colón in Buenos Aires stands out among his Orchestra tours. According to Mr. Haigh, its "fabulous acoustics and beauty" make it one of the world's foremost concert halls. His admiration of Latin American culture extends beyond his regard for the Teatro, however. Of Cuban descent on his mother's side, he thoroughly enjoys Latin American and Spanish folk music and speaks Spanish.

Mr. Haigh is listed in *Who's Who in American Music* and *The International Who's Who* for his musical accomplishments. In addition to his artistic activities, he enjoys jogging, playing racquetball, collecting art, and learning new languages.

Scott Haigh
Bass
1978

Anthony Knight, assistant principal bass, began to play the piano at age seven and the bass after the fifth grade. Mr. Knight is a native of Indiana and received his degree from Ball State University in Muncie. He played with the World Youth Symphony at Interlochen while in high school, and this experience prompted him to make a career of music. Before moving to Cleveland, Mr. Knight played with the Colorado Philharmonic, Berkshire Music Center Orchestra at Tanglewood, and the Denver Symphony Orchestra.

Mr. Knight teaches double bass privately and at Baldwin-Wallace College Conservatory. He has published an article in the *Instrumentalist* entitled "Teaching the Young Bassist: A Private Teacher's Outlook."

Listening to bluegrass music, woodworking, and golfing are favorite diversions for Mr. Knight, when he can find an unoccupied moment. He and his wife Martha are kept quite busy with their young children Andrea and Scott.

Anthony Knight
Bass
1974

Jacques Posell is neither the only professional musician in his family nor the only author. Among his written works is "The Double Bass in Chamber Music," published in *The Instrumentalist*.

His wife Elsa is a children's author and librarian, whose many works include *This is an Orchestra*, *Russian Composers*, and *American Composers*. Their son George is an assistant conductor of the Metropolitan Opera Company. Their daughter Annette is in public relations at WGBH in Boston.

Mr. Posell was born in Paris and grew up in the United States. He began playing the violin at age seven. "I gave it up three years later, because I was a poor student and did not particularly like to practice," he recalls. After attending a New York concert as a high school student, he decided he wanted to play the oboe. His high school did not own an oboe, however, and the orchestra director offered him a bass instead.

Mr. Posell attended Curtis and studied with Anton Torello, principal bassist of the Philadelphia Orchestra. Mr. Posell served as principal bassist of the National Symphony for five years and spent three summers with the Hollywood Bowl Orchestra and twelve summers with the Central City Opera in Colorado. He was principal in The Cleveland Orchestra from 1939 to 1967. He has taught at Oberlin (for twenty-seven years), CIM, and the Cleveland Music School Settlement.

The Posells appreciate Cleveland's affordability and comfort, in spite of the severe winters. Mr. Posell is an accomplished photographer and enjoys touring with his camera.

Jacques Posell
Bass
1936

During its first thirteen years, The Cleveland Orchestra was all male. In 1931 the first woman joined and today, fifteen percent of the Orchestra members are women.

Thomas Sepulveda

Bass

1967

Although **Thomas Sepulveda** had no formal musical training as a child, he began playing bass in dance bands and jazz groups during his high school years. He still finds his career simultaneously challenging and rewarding. "I believe I can always learn and improve my musical skills," he commented.

Mr. Sepulveda received a bachelor's degree in teaching from the University of North Colorado, but concentrated on music thereafter. He earned a master's degree from Eastman and at the same time gained his first professional orchestral experience in the Rochester Philharmonic.

Mr. Sepulveda's tenure with The Cleveland Orchestra was interrupted twice. He was drafted into the Army Band at West Point after his first season with the Orchestra. In 1978 he began a three-year position as principal bassist of the Kansas City Philharmonic.

He has written pieces for solo bass and has performed his own music for small audiences. His travels with the Orchestra have often provided him with inspiration and unique experiences. He particularly savors his memories of climbing into the Grand Canyon, alone and at night.

Mr. Sepulveda's other interests include roller skating, which he took up one summer while performing in the Grand Tetons Music Festival in Wyoming, sailing, and gardening.

Laura Okuniewski
Harp
1980

Laura Okuniewski believes that "everything in your life contributes to how you make music." When she backpacks and birdwatches, the enrichment she gains from these experiences is reflected in her playing.

A Detroit native, whose parents claim that she begged for a harp even as a preschooler, Ms. Okuniewski finally began lessons in the third grade. This was after she again told her mother, during the funeral of John Kennedy, that she wanted to play the instrument they heard on the broadcast: a harp that played "Greensleeves."

She began studying with Mary Bartlett and attended high school at the Interlochen Arts Academy, where she worked with Elisa Dickon. During the summers Ms. Okuniewski traveled to the Salzedo Summer Harp Colony in Camden, Maine, to study with Alice Chalifoux, former Cleveland Orchestra principal harpist.

Ms. Okuniewski next enrolled at CIM and again worked with Miss Chalifoux. During those years she attended Cleveland Orchestra concerts faithfully. She has been principal harpist of the orchestras in Xalapa, Mexico, and Charleston, West Virginia, and has soloed with the Suburban Symphony and the CIM Orchestra. In 1981, during her senior year at CIM, she was appointed assistant principal harpist of The Cleveland Orchestra.

Ms. Okuniewski listens to all kinds of music and particularly enjoys playing with Reconnaissance, Cleveland's contemporary music group. She teaches in a private studio and practices the Salzedo technique of harp playing.

The Orchestra's tour to Japan was especially enjoyable for her. "Magical moments do happen on stage, even with a piece played many, many times, because Orchestra members play for themselves and for each other," she observes. She finds Cleveland's Metropark System and University Circle's cultural concentration unique, and credits her friends with making Cleveland a good place to live.

Lisa Wellbaum (signature)

Lisa Wellbaum
Harp
1974

Maintaining the delicate balance between the demands of a professional musician and those of mother of two young children comes naturally to **Lisa Wellbaum**. She grew up in a musical family: her mother is a harpist and her father plays piccolo and is personnel manager of the Cincinnati Symphony. Ms. Wellbaum started to play the piano at age three, and the harp and flute at age ten. Her parents were her tutors during her early years of study.

As a teenager Ms. Wellbaum never dreamed she would be a professional musician, for drama and languages were her primary interests. At that time, however, she spent her summers in Camden, Maine, studying the harp with former Cleveland Orchestra member, Alice Chalifoux. Along with her mother, she credits Miss Chalifoux as being most influential in her choice of a musical career. Miss Chalifoux also encouraged her to come to Cleveland, and Ms. Wellbaum subsequently graduated from CIM.

Her professional career includes positions as principal harpist of the New Orleans Philharmonic, Winnipeg Symphony, and Santa Fe Opera as well as performances with the orchestras of Cincinnati, Pittsburgh, Indianapolis, and Milwaukee.

Ms. Wellbaum is principal harpist of The Cleveland Orchestra, a position she inherited from Miss Chalifoux. She is married to principal cellist Stephen Geber, and they have a three-year-old daughter, Stephanie, who already shows musical tendencies, and a daughter Lauren, born in 1983.

The excitement of touring with The Cleveland Orchestra also has its drawbacks, as both parents must leave small children at home. Nevertheless, Ms. Wellbaum finds that traveling with the Orchestra on its international tours has been one of the greatest experiences of her life, although she has to travel with a full supply of strings and pedal rods. She has always enjoyed meeting harpists, both American and foreign, in each port of call.

Ms. Wellbaum's favorite composers are Mahler and Puccini; her musical preference is opera. She has taught the Salzedo method of harp playing, espoused by Miss Chalifoux. She feels that aspiring harpists should have some background in piano before beginning the harp.

Ms. Wellbaum owns two harps, one for use at home, and one for Severance Hall. Her hobbies are photography and keeping scrapbooks.

The Cleveland Orchestra Chorus

Robert Page 13   M. Seredick 124

Weiner 118   Miller 117   Mar 11

Kofshy 111   Boyd 109   De 11

Anderson 112

Jones 119   Bishop 113

Powers 101   Schmitter 102

Zetzer 95   Peterson 94   Johnson 93   Co 9

Hebert 87   Rautenberg 86   Aarons 84   Kh

Brown Berman 18

Wellbaum 81

Skuniewski 80

Polyakin Wolfson Deninzon 22

Koch 31

B. Siegel 40

Voldnich 45   G. Siegel 41

Freilich 25   Epstein 24

Warner 46

Straum 43

Benkovic 17   Raffaelli 36

Gad

Samuels Tishhoff S. Majeske 44   34   35

Zimmer Loebel Chusid Furiyoshi 48   33   26

Kardos Eichhorn Snader 30   23   42

de Granda 21

M. Setzer 39   Llinas 32

Goldschmidt 28   E. Setzer 38

Christo

Yoel Levi 12

Christop

Altschulen 16

Moore 29

D. Majeske 15

The Clevelan

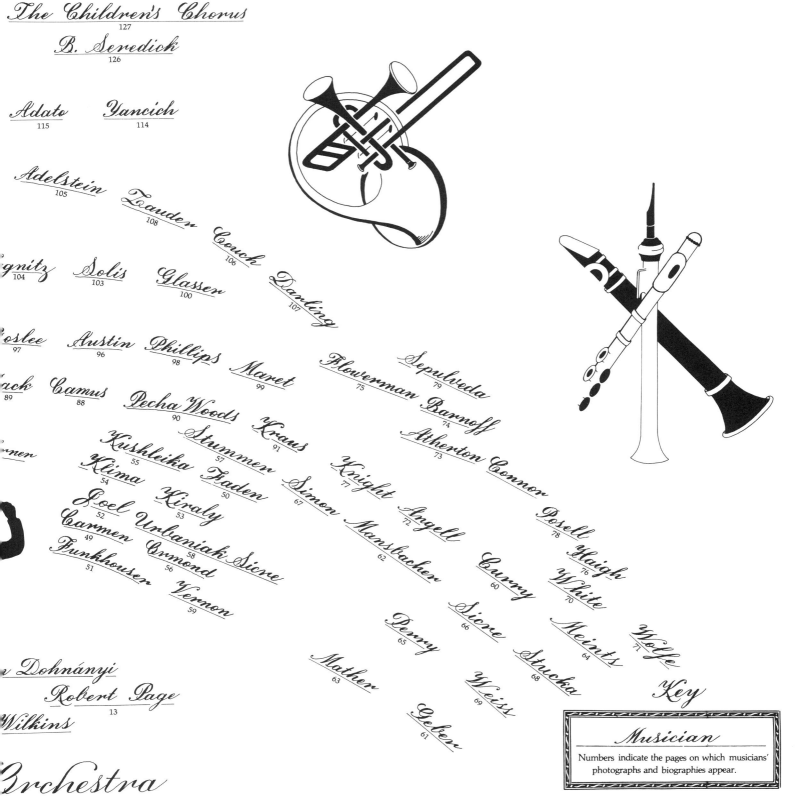

The Children's Chorus
127

B. Seredick
126

Adato
115

Yancich
114

Adelstein
105

Zauder
108

Couch
106

Darling
107

gnitz
104

Solis
103

Glasser
100

oslee
97

Austin
96

Phillips
98

Maret
99

Flowerman
75

Sepulveda
79

ack
89

Camus
88

Pecha
90

Woods

Kraus
91

Barnoff
74

Atherton
73

Connor

Posell
78

rner

Kushleika
55

Stummer
57

Simon
67

Knight
77

Angell
72

Cunny
60

Haigh
76

Klima
54

Faden
50

White
70

Poel
52

Kiraly
53

Mansbacher
62

Sicre
66

Meints

Wolfe
71

Carmen
49

Urbaniak
58

Sicre

Stucka
68

Funkhouser
51

Ormond
56

Vernon
59

Penny
65

Weiss
69

Dohnányi

Robert Page
13

Mather
63

Wilkins

Geben
61

Key

Orchestra

Musician

Numbers indicate the pages on which musicians'
photographs and biographies appear.

Her parents' love of music first stimulated **Martha Aarons'** own interest. She began her musical studies with piano before she took up the flute in the fourth grade. By the time she was in high school she attended as many concerts as possible, once fitting two Philadelphia Orchestra concerts into the same day.

Ms. Aarons feels fortunate to have had the opportunity, while still in high school, to play in some of her native Los Angeles' many youth and community orchestras and a woodwind quintet. Initially the motivation was partly social: "Playing in orchestras gave me a niche outside of school, where I hadn't really found one," she recalls, "but it quickly developed into a passion for orchestral playing that has remained constant."

Ms. Aarons attended CIM, Juilliard, and UCLA (where she took mostly nonmusic courses). Prior to joining The Cleveland Orchestra she was the principal flutist and a frequent soloist with the North Carolina Symphony. She taught at Duke University, the University of North Carolina at Chapel Hill, and at the Eastern Music Festival, and is currently on the faculties of CIM and the Blossom Festival School.

Her approach to teaching is quite personal and varies somewhat with each individual student. Ms. Aarons feels that students should augment their private lessons by listening to great orchestral and solo performances and emulating (as opposed to imitating) their strengths.

Her other interests include reading, travel, sewing, and food—both its preparation and consumption.

Martha Aarons
Flute
1981

Jeffrey Khaner

Jeffrey Khaner

Flute

1982

Although **Jeffrey Khaner** remembers having an unexplainable desire to study the flute, his future with the instrument was determined somewhat by chance. When his high school decided to start a band, he went out of his way to sign up for the flute. Yet when the band director announced that no one had requested to play tuba, Mr. Khaner and one other student volunteered. The band director chose the other student to fill the vacancy, and Mr. Khaner's career as a flutist began.

His parents were very supportive of his musical aspirations, but did not force him to practice. Although his older brother is a cellist with the Edmonton Symphony, Mr. Khaner insists that his desire to pursue music as a career was not influenced by his brother's example but was his own decision. After studying with Jeanne Baxtresser in Montreal, Mr. Khaner went through a period of intense study and career preparation at Juilliard, working with Julius Baker. He feels that this time spent "with blinders on" was imperative to his musical development, and that all musicians who are truly serious about their music undergo similar experiences.

Before coming to Cleveland as principal, Mr. Khaner was principal flutist of the Atlantic Symphony in his native Canada and the Mostly Mozart Festival in New York City, as well as co-principal in the Pittsburgh Symphony.

Currently Mr. Khaner spends a great deal of time learning new music in order to familiarize himself with the Orchestra's vast repertoire, and teaching at CIM. When Mr. Khaner does find time to relax, he enjoys visiting the Art Museum and exploring Cleveland and its surroundings.

John Rautenberg comes from an extremely musical Cleveland family. His father, the late Theodore Rautenberg, was a violinist with The Cleveland Orchestra, and his stepmother is a pianist. His uncle Maurice Sharp was principal flutist of The Cleveland Orchestra for fifty years, and his daughter is a violin major at Indiana University.

Mr. Rautenberg plays several musical instruments in addition to the flute. These include the piano, which he learned to play as a child, saxophone, which he relied upon in college as a means of earning money, and a harpsichord that he built. His childhood ambition to play the flute began at a Cleveland Orchestra Twilight Concert he attended in the third grade. He remembers being fascinated by the flute solo and deciding that he would like to play the flute professionally.

He began his flute studies with Robert Morris at age ten and later studied with Mr. Sharp from the sixth through twelfth grades. While at Oberlin he studied with Robert Willoughby. Mr. Rautenberg graduated from Oberlin with a degree in music education and spent three years as a member of the Indianapolis Symphony before joining the Orchestra. He also has played with the Santa Fe Opera and the orchestras of North Carolina and Chautauqua. He was appointed associate principal flutist in 1968.

Although Mr. Rautenberg has taught at Oberlin, CIM, and the University of Akron, he now teaches only privately and in master classes.

Mr. Rautenberg is interested and excels in a number of nonmusical pursuits. He has built three sailboats, he and his wife sail regularly on Lake Erie, and he has sailed solo across the Lake. In recent years he has taken up figure skating and cross-country skiing.

John Rautenberg
Flute
1961

William Hebert

Piccolo

1947

William Hebert's musical beginnings are as interesting as the man himself. Following a childhood bout with tuberculosis, he began flute lessons because his mother decided they would provide excellent therapy for strengthening his lungs. His first musical instrument was a military fife, which he played for five weeks before purchasing a flute. He began playing the piccolo when he received one as a grammar school graduation present.

After World War II, Mr. Hebert attended Juilliard on the GI Bill. While there he studied with Arthur Lora, and later with James Pappoutsakis of the Boston Symphony Orchestra. He played piccolo and flute in the New York City Center Symphony, Opera, and Ballet, before joining The Cleveland Orchestra.

Mr. Hebert and his wife Olive have seven children. Two of their sons, Britton and Martin, are professional musicians, and four others are also instrumentalists.

One of Mr. Hebert's great and continuing loves is a farm in Chardon which he and Mrs. Hebert purchased during the 1950s as a place for family camping expeditions. Although the Department of Agriculture said that it could not be done, the Heberts dug a pond and stocked it with fish. They also planted pine seedlings, which have since grown into a forest, and cultivate a variety of fruits and vegetables using organic farming techniques. Mr. Hebert has published several articles on ecology and farming, including one in *Mother Earth News.*

Partly because of the influence of the younger generation of Heberts, Mr. Hebert's musical tastes are catholic. His favorite composers are Mozart (if he is listening in the audience) and J. S. Bach (if he is performing). His favorite major choral works are Bach's *Mass in B Minor* and Verdi's *Requiem.*

Mr. Hebert is a part-time member of the music faculty at Baldwin-Wallace College, where he has taught since 1950. He has transcribed and arranged compositions for symphonic wind ensemble and woodwind quintet. As a soloist, he has appeared with The Cleveland Orchestra, Akron Symphony, Cleveland Philharmonic, Cleveland Women's Orchestra, and at the Baldwin-Wallace Bach Festival.

Elizabeth Camus

Elizabeth Camus
Oboe
1979

When she began to study music at the age of nine, it seemed only natural that **Elizabeth Camus** would play the trumpet, just as her four brothers had before her. Ms. Camus labels the year she spent studying the trumpet "a disaster," and she recalls one fateful day when, at the age of eleven, she heard a high school student playing the oboe. She was taken with the sound, and decided to learn to play the instrument herself.

By the age of fourteen, Ms. Camus, a native of New Orleans, was studying with Cleveland Orchestra principal John Mack, who was at that time principal oboist of the New Orleans Symphony.

After graduation, Ms. Camus came to Cleveland to study with Mr. Mack at CIM. However, the feeling that being a musician was perhaps "not enough of a contribution" caused her to change fields, and for two and a half years she was a psychology major at Cleveland State University. Ultimately she realized that music was "apparently a thing which chose me, rather than my choosing it," and returned to the oboe full time, teaching and freelancing in the Cleveland area. She left in 1972 to assume the principal chair of the San Antonio Symphony and subsequently served six years with the Atlanta Symphony, the last two as principal, before joining The Cleveland Orchestra.

Ms. Camus finds her career in music to be both emotionally and intellectually satisfying. She enjoys dealing in "what amounts to another language" and its effects on the emotions, and she especially relishes the challenge of trying to do something perfectly, as is required in the performance of music. Ms. Camus feels very strongly about the teaching aspect of her career. "All children should study music, in one context or another —as a means of expression, of course, but also as a discipline, as a means of understanding structure and form, and as a means of developing an approach to other mental tasks."

Ms. Camus also plays with an Orchestra quintet which donates its services to the annual WCLV Marathon. She teaches at Case Western Reserve University and privately. In her free time she enjoys crossword puzzles, gardening, and cooking.

John Mack deeply loves music. He views music as more than an academic discipline, and he feels that one must never lose sight of "the coursing of blood in the music itself."

One of his most delightful childhood memories is that of his mother, who sang and played piano, letting him choose from her repertoire the piece she would play while he went to bed. Much to her joy she discovered that, like her own mother, her son had perfect pitch. When he was in the sixth grade, Mr. Mack was the only student to recognize the oboe and English horn when a record of orchestral instruments was played. The music teacher immediately decided that Mr. Mack must play the oboe, and his fate was sealed.

Mr. Mack began to play a pawnshop oboe which his father had bought almost as a curiosity. Despite a slow beginning and a tendency to be stiff-fingered, Mr. Mack mastered the instrument. He credits his success to strong willpower, and he recalls his father's helpful advice: "Son, do not take no for an answer from inanimate objects."

While in high school Mr. Mack studied with Bruno Labate, principal oboist of the New York Philharmonic, and Marcel Tabuteau, the premiere oboe teacher in this country. Mr. Mack's high school friends expected him to go into science, but although he won prizes in science and physics, he found music to be more attractive. He attended Juilliard, where, at the age of nineteen, he played first oboe with the Juilliard Orchestra. He then attended Curtis for an additional three years of study with Marcel Tabuteau.

Before coming to Cleveland as principal Mr. Mack was principal oboist of the Sadler's Wells Ballet, the New Orleans Symphony, and the National Symphony.

Mr. Mack teaches at CIM and privately. For the past eight summers he has hosted the John Mack Oboe Camp near Little Switzerland, North Carolina. Here he teaches some seventy oboe students, ranging from teenagers to senior citizens.

A transcript of an address, *Effective Guidance to Young Oboists*, given by Mr. Mack to the International Society for Double Reeds in 1973, has been reprinted several times. He is generally acknowledged to be the best reedmaker in the country.

Mr. Mack's wife Anne is a violist with the Akron Symphony. They have three children. When his schedule permits, Mr. Mack loves to play golf. One of his dreams is that "400 years from now, Mozart will still live."

John Mack
Oboe
1965

Pamela Pecha Woods
Oboe
1978

Pamela Pecha Woods was deeply involved in music throughout her childhood. At an early age she began to study piano. Later she played clarinet, served as student conductor of the high school orchestra and chorus, and seriously studied ballet.

Her father Emerich Pecha played the oboe in the Pittsburgh and Houston Symphonies and, as she heard her father practice, Ms. Pecha Woods learned to love the oboe. When the high school band needed someone to play that instrument, she volunteered. In her mid-teens, Ms. Pecha Woods began to consider music as a career. She was motivated by her love of music, as well as a desire to be one of the first women to play the oboe successfully.

Ms. Pecha Woods studied at CIM from 1969 to 1973 with Orchestra principal John Mack. After playing with the orchestras of Cincinnati, San Antonio, and Mexico, the Orchestra of the Americas, and the Baltimore Symphony, Ms. Pecha Woods joined The Cleveland Orchestra as assistant principal. She was the first woman to be appointed to the woodwind section of the Orchestra and the first woman oboist to gain a position in one of the top five orchestras in the country.

Ms. Pecha Woods plays with the Cleveland Woodwind Quintet. She has enjoyed appearing as soloist at the Eastern Music Festival, CIM, and the Severance Chamber Series. When she was with the Baltimore Symphony, Ms. Pecha Woods conducted that group in a children's concert. She enjoys conducting and views it as a possible future pursuit.

Currently Ms. Pecha Woods' time is devoted to orchestral playing, giving private oboe instruction, and mothering her infant daughter, Melissa. Ms. Pecha Woods is married to Robert Woods, the co-owner and executive vice president of Telarc Records and the winner of Grammy Awards as "Classical Producer of the Year" in 1980 and 1982.

Felix Kraus
English Horn
1963

At the age of six **Felix Kraus** began to study the violin in Austria, after his family arranged lessons to help an impoverished violin teacher who had fled to Vienna from Hitler's Germany. The annexation of Austria by Germany caused his parents to send him to England, and it was only as a teenager that Mr. Kraus was reunited with them in the United States.

Mr. Kraus then took up the tuba and became one of the best players in the school band. Because the high school orchestra was too small to include a tuba, its director suggested that Mr. Kraus take up the oboe. Although unusual, the transfer was not terribly difficult, for the tuba and oboe are both double-embouchure instruments; that is, they require equal strength in both lips.

While still in his teens, Mr. Kraus joined the Houston Symphony as second oboist. The following year he was admitted to Curtis as a scholarship student of Marcel Tabuteau, whom he credits as being most influential in his musical education.

The Korean War brought him to Washington, D.C., where he served for two and a half years as English hornist of the U.S. Army Band. During this time he began to study mathematics and after his military service enrolled as a math major at the University of California at Berkeley. The pull of music proved too strong, however. A year later he was invited to become principal oboist of the Portland (now Oregon) Symphony.

Mr. Kraus spent the next three years as principal oboist of the National Symphony before coming to Cleveland. He was appointed solo English hornist in 1979 and has appeared as soloist with the Orchestra in both the regular and Friday morning subscription series at Severance Hall and at Oberlin as well. He has performed works by Mozart, Reicha, Copland, and Donizetti.

Mr. Kraus and the Coventry Chamber Players presented the world premiere of the Quintet for English Horn and Strings written by Paul Turok for Mr. Kraus. As an oboist, he has played the Cimarosa Oboe Concerto with the Orchestra at Cleveland's Public Auditorium. He has played many works at the Cleveland Museum of Art with Orchestra members, including oboe concertos of Mozart, Frigyes Hidas, and Vaughan Williams.

Mr. Kraus has served on the faculties of the University of Akron, Case Western Reserve University, and the Summer Music Experience in Hudson. His hobbies include the study of foreign languages and bicycling.

It was while lying in bed at night listening to his mother, a piano teacher, play the piano that **Franklin Cohen's** love of music began. At age eight he picked a clarinet off the music store's shelf and thus began his musical career.

Born in New York City, Mr. Cohen was raised in a family where music was appreciated. He received a bachelor of music degree from Juilliard. From the time he earned the distinction of being the only clarinetist ever to win the first prize in the International Munich Competition, he has pursued an active career as a soloist, recitalist, chamber musician, and orchestral artist.

He was solo clarinetist of the American Symphony Orchestra under Stokowski and held the same position in the Baltimore Symphony before joining The Cleveland Orchestra as principal clarinetist. His 1968 Munich Competition prize-winning performance of the Mozart Concerto with the Bavarian Radio Orchestra was one of the highlights of his career. Mr. Cohen loves playing chamber music, especially with many of his close friends. He is a regular member of the Santa Fe Chamber Music Festival.

He has taught at Juilliard, Aspen, and the Peabody Conservatory of Music, and is currently chairman of the clarinet departments at CIM and Blossom Festival School. To young persons interested in pursuing careers in music, Mr. Cohen advises, "set fundamental musical goals instead of only instrumental goals, work hard, and keep focused on what you want."

An early riser, Mr. Cohen fills his days with practicing and rehearsals, but there is always time to share with his wife and four-year-old daughter Dianna. His wife Lynette is the principal bassoonist of the Ohio Chamber Orchestra and Akron Symphony. Physical fitness is also an important part of his life: running, biking, and cross-country skiing are favorite activities. He is a Porsche enthusiast and collector of antique Navajo tapestries and rugs as well.

Franklin Cohen
Clarinet
1976

Theodore Johnson is a native of Chicago. He graduated from a high school that produced many prominent musicians, including several current members of the Chicago Symphony Orchestra, one member besides himself of The Cleveland Orchestra, and the jazz great Benny Goodman.

He started playing the clarinet at the age of nine at the request of his parents, who felt his interest in sports was becoming too strong. What was intended as a meaningful extracurricular activity eventually developed into a successful career.

Prior to college, Mr. Johnson studied with Jerome Stowell, a clarinetist with the Chicago Symphony Orchestra, and upon graduation from high school he continued his studies with Mr. Stowell at DePaul University. After receiving his bachelor of music degree in clarinet he joined the Kansas City Philharmonic and played with the Santa Fe Opera during the summers. Other engagements included performances with the Chicago Symphony, Casals Festival, Kansas City Lyric Opera, Ravinia Festival, and Grant Park Orchestras. While in Kansas City, Mr. Johnson nearly decided to abandon music for medicine. However, his appointment to The Cleveland Orchestra intervened. He also plays E-flat clarinet with the Orchestra.

Mr. Johnson enjoys teaching. In Kansas City he was director of woodwinds for the Kansas City, Kansas, school system and he now serves on faculties at CIM, Cleveland State University, and Summer Music Experience in Hudson.

Of special interest to him are the muscular problems related to the tension involved in musical performance. He has devised several relaxation techniques to help relieve these problems.

Mr. Johnson enjoys chamber music and currently plays with the Cleveland Octet. Other interests include photography and power-boating. He spends most of his free summer hours on a twenty-six-foot Skiffcraft.

Theodore Johnson
Clarinet
1959

Thomas Peterson
Clarinet
1963

Thomas Peterson's mother had hoped he would play the piano, but he chose the clarinet at age ten in order to have some experience in ensemble playing, and also as a means of terminating piano study. He studied with Lee Hardesty and Harold Wright in Washington, D.C., during his high school and college years and credits both these gentlemen with influencing his career decision.

Mr. Peterson graduated with distinction from Eastman, where he studied with Rufus Arey and Stanley Hasty, and was awarded a B.M. degree and the performer's certificate in clarinet. He played with the Buffalo Philharmonic for six years and served there as principal for three years prior to coming to Cleveland. He is assistant principal clarinetist and saxophonist with the Orchestra.

His wife Barbara is a flutist who has often played with the Orchestra, both locally and abroad. They enjoy travel, particularly when they accompany the Orchestra. The 1965 tour of the Soviet Union and Europe remains Mr. Peterson's most outstanding travel memory.

He enjoys listening to jazz and short wave radio. His current interests involve his home computer, investing, and economics.

When the twelve-year-old **Alfred Zetzer** walked up to a Cleveland school band director and told him he wanted to play a musical instrument, the director looked closely at his mouth, said "good teeth," and handed Mr. Zetzer his first clarinet. He loved the music it made and found practicing a joy, coping easily with the fingering demands of the instrument despite his left-handedness. He later studied at CIM and graduated with the school's first bachelor of music degree in clarinet. His teachers Daniel Bonade and Carl Kuhlman were important in his musical development.

Mr. Zetzer organized and conducted the Cleveland Children's Symphony and was one of the original organizers of the Cleveland Philharmonic. Before joining The Cleveland Orchestra as bass clarinetist, he was solo clarinetist with the Ballets Russes de Monte Carlo Orchestra, Kansas City Philharmonic, Pittsburgh Symphony, and San Antonio Symphony. His thirty-five year tenure with the Orchestra has been most enjoyable. He continues to play the clarinet in addition to bass clarinet, and he particularly enjoys performing works by Wagner and Strauss.

Mr. Zetzer has taught privately in Cleveland and was on the faculties of Kent State University and the Cleveland Music School Settlement. He currently teaches at CIM. He and his wife Edith enjoy collecting Spode china and antique clarinets.

Alfred Zetzer
Bass Clarinet
1949

Although Cleveland Orchestra musicians studied at many prominent educational institutions, forty-eight attended either CIM, Juilliard, or Eastman. CIM alone trained twenty-one Orchestra members.

Phillip Austin began his musical career in elementary school when he joined the school band. In junior high the band director needed a bassoonist and Mr. Austin, being a "joiner," accepted the challenge, although he did not know what a bassoon was.

Mr. Austin was committed to his music and practiced faithfully, although he did not come from a home where classical music was appreciated. He became involved in community and youth orchestras in the Detroit area, and since there was no orchestra in his high school, he continued to play with the school band.

During the summers when he was sixteen, seventeen, and nineteen, Mr. Austin played with the Meadow Brook School of Music Orchestra. His experiences with this school of the Detroit Symphony Orchestra were memorable, because during two of these summers he played under James Levine.

At Wayne State University in Detroit, Mr. Austin majored in music education and planned to pursue a teaching career if he "was not good enough to play professionally." Upon graduation, he put himself to the test by moving to New York City. He freelanced and "practically starved to death." However, at the age of twenty-three he was hired by the Detroit Symphony Orchestra. He played there for nine and a half years before coming to Cleveland.

Mr. Austin recalls that Charles Sirard, retired principal bassoonist of the Detroit Symphony Orchestra, was influential in his career. Mr. Sirard helped Mr. Austin purchase his first and present bassoon, a 1960 Heckel. Prior to that time, he had played a rented or borrowed instrument.

Mr. Austin has studied with Lyell Lindsey, Charles Sirard, William Kaplan, and Elias Carmen. He also has taken lessons at the Mozarteum in Salzburg and studied reed making with Louis Skinner in Maine. He currently teaches at the Cleveland Music School Settlement and plays with other Orchestra members in the Cleveland Wind Quintet.

Mr. Austin feels that culture and the arts will always exist, for "there is more to life than just its sustenance. Culture and art are reasonable and lasting." His hobbies include designing and making stained glass windows and collecting miniature bassoon figurines. He and his wife Rhonda have one child, Sammy, and also enjoy the renovation of their vintage 1918 Cleveland Heights home.

Phillip E. Austin

Phillip Austin
Bassoon
1981

Music was always encouraged in **George Goslee's** family. His brothers played the piano and jazz, and when one brother came home from school looking for a volunteer to play the bassoon, Mr. Goslee's career was determined. Born in western Ohio, he attended Eastman, where Vincent Pezzi had a major influence on his career.

Prior to joining The Cleveland Orchestra as principal bassoonist, Mr. Goslee played with the New Orleans Symphony, the Rochester Philharmonic, the Indianapolis Symphony, and the Philadelphia Orchestra. He has played under many of the world's great conductors, but his most memorable experience was with Toscanini. Mr. Goslee was new to the musical world at the time, and it was a thrill to work with such a legend.

Mr. Goslee enjoys performing and listening to the works of Mozart. He finds European audiences warm and very responsive, and fondly remembers a European tour with George Szell when the audience "practically brought the house down with their enthusiasm."

Mr. Goslee teaches at CIM and feels a responsibility to develop a total person, not a narrow musician. He encourages fine mechanics and artistic habits, as well as a well-rounded individuality.

When Mr. Goslee is not performing, practicing, or teaching, he pursues his interests in photography, books, boating, and wine. Music remains important in the Goslee home; all four children are musicians.

George Goslee
Bassoon
1943

Ronald Phillips, assistant principal bassoonist, is best characterized by his pride in and love for Cleveland. Born in Illinois and reared in Cleveland, he feels that the city is a great place to live, with its vast array of cultural activities, neighborhoods, and fine park systems.

Mr. Phillips started playing the bassoon after scoring high on a music aptitude test at the age of thirteen. Intrigued by the unknown instrument, he began playing in a school band. Within one year he began lessons with a private teacher and was determined to make a career in music.

Before attending Eastman, Mr. Phillips studied with Orchestra principal George Goslee. He feels the time he spent with Mr. Goslee played a major role in his early musical life, developing both his skills and his love of music. He has played with the Rochester Philharmonic, U.S. Navy Band, and New Orleans Philharmonic.

Currently on the faculty at Baldwin-Wallace College, Mr. Phillips has always been involved in teaching. All four of his children were exposed to various instruments, and although none is a professional musician, the experience "gave them a fine appreciation of music and music-making."

Mr. Phillips believes the American orchestra system is a strong one. The extreme competitiveness for every single spot results in a high level of excellence among musicians. "With the vast improvement of teaching techniques, there are many more fine musicians for every position," he observed. He thus encourages his students to develop skills in other areas, as well as music.

His other interests are gardening and antiques.

Ronald Phillips
Bassoon
1960

Stanley Maret
Contra-bassoon
1962

Stanley Maret was born in Joplin, Missouri. His earliest exposure to music was hearing his father's Wagner recordings and broadcasts of the Metropolitan Opera and the New York Philharmonic. Wagner never became one of his favorite composers, but he recalls that "Tchaikovsky symphonies deeply affected me very early in life." Mr. Maret began piano lessons at the age of five and later played the trombone and bassoon.

While he was growing up, popular music was dominated by the Big Bands. After high school, Mr. Maret joined a traveling dance band as a vocalist and pianist, but soon became disillusioned with the life and realized he would be happier as a classical musician. Strongly motivated by his admiration for Rachmaninoff and George Gershwin, he recalls wanting to be "like Rachmaninoff: a composer, pianist, and conductor." This youthful fantasy, as he now describes it, gave way to serious study of the bassoon.

Mr. Maret received a B.M. degree from Eastman, where he studied bassoon with Vincent Pezzi and composition with Burrill Phillips. He played second bassoon with the Denver Symphony for six years, during which time he earned a master of music degree in composition from the University of Colorado at Boulder. Following a year of teaching, Mr. Maret accepted a fellowship at the University of Illinois and spent four years as a doctoral candidate in composition and philosophy there.

Mr. Maret came to Ohio in 1961 to teach bassoon and theory at Oberlin. While he was a member of the Oberlin faculty, George Szell invited him to audition for the contra-bassoon position with The Cleveland Orchestra and engaged him for that chair.

Mr. Maret very much enjoys his work with The Cleveland Orchestra. He cherishes the close friendships he has formed over the years and loves international touring. He particularly enjoys learning and using as much as he can of the languages of the countries he visits and photographing children wherever the Orchestra travels.

Mr. Maret teaches bassoon and coaches woodwind ensembles at the Summer Music Experience in Hudson, which he describes as "one of the joys of my life." His wife Anne works at the Case Western Reserve University Kulas Music Library, and their son Bryan, a mathematician currently working as a computer programmer in Minneapolis, is a serious amateur flutist.

An airport-closing blizzard did not deter **David Glasser's** travel from San Diego to an audition with The Cleveland Orchestra in January of 1978. He joined the Orchestra the following month and has grown to enjoy Cleveland's changing seasons. He is restoring a house that is home to an array of musical equipment and his Russian Blue cat, Nicolai.

Arts enthusiasts, Mr. Glasser's parents strongly encouraged their four children to develop their artistic abilities. Each began piano in elementary school, and concert- and museum-going were regular childhood activities. Mr. Glasser started piano in the fourth grade and decided to play horn the next year. The horn is an unwieldy instrument, and his instructor started him on the trumpet before moving him to the horn six months later.

Mr. Glasser cites Ralph Pyle, of the Los Angeles Philharmonic, with whom he studied while at the California Institute of the Arts, as his most influential teacher. Mr. Pyle not only provided excellent technical instruction but also guidance on the management of a career in music. Mr. Glasser graduated with his B.F.A. in 1975. He continued his education at the University of California at Irvine and the New College Summer Music Festival and served as assistant conductor for various brass ensembles at all three institutions. He attended the Fellowship Program at Tanglewood in 1976 and also studied with James Decker, Dale Clevenger, Paul Ingraham, and Charles Kavalovski.

Mr. Glasser has performed with the San Diego Symphony, San Diego Opera, Los Angeles Radio Orchestra, Monday Evening Concerts Contemporary Ensemble, UCLA Contemporary Ensemble, Mount St. Mary's Symphony Orchestra, and Ventura Symphony. He currently serves as assistant principal in the Orchestra and plays with the Severance Brass Quintet and Cleveland Octet.

He has taught at the University of California at Irvine, Hidden Valley Music Seminars, Lakeland Community College, and the Summer Music Experience in Hudson, as well as given master classes. Mr. Glasser was horn soloist in Thea Musgrave's *Space Play* and in Mozart's Horn Concertos Nos. 2 and 4 with Mount St. Mary's Symphony Orchestra and New College Summer Music Festival Orchestra. He also has given recitals on both horn and piano.

Mr. Glasser plays a Conn 8-D horn, made in 1965, and also owns a C.F. Schmidt made in 1915 and a natural horn made by Gottlob Eschenbach in 1811.

David Glasser
Horn
1978

A native of Buffalo, **Jeffrey Powers** began his musical studies with piano at age nine. When his family moved to Texas one year later, the "upright" did not go. Mr. Powers' studies thus were interrupted until a high school music theory teacher encouraged him to play an instrument. It was then that he took up French horn.

He received his B.A. with honors in music from Austin College and M.M. in horn from CIM. Mr. Powers studied with Cleveland Orchestra member Albert Schmitter, Myron Bloom, James London, and Roy Waas. He has previously held positions with La Filarmonica de Caracas, the New Jersey Symphony Orchestra, and the Hong Kong Philharmonic. Mr. Powers currently plays solo horn with the William Appling Orchestra and is a member of the Cleveland Wind Quartet.

Although he enjoys playing symphonic music of all composers and periods, Mr. Powers would like to see contemporary and modern works given more attention. As a listener, he enjoys chamber music, opera (particularly that of Puccini), and jazz.

Since coming to Cleveland, Mr. Powers has been a horn instructor and chamber music coach for the Summer Music Experience in Hudson. His advice to aspiring musicians is: "Practice regularly; remember the importance of discipline; always be your own worst critic in order to grow; and most importantly, realize and always remember that the motivation to pursue a professional career in music should be a deep-seated love of music."

Mr. Powers enjoys running and bicycling, as well as the visual and other fine arts.

Jeffrey Powers
Horn
1980

As early as the third grade **Albert Schmitter's** original musical goal was to play trumpet in the school band. By the time he reached high school, however, the only available position for the Painesville native was French horn.

Initially influenced by the band director, Otto Schmidt, Mr. Schmitter feels that each of his teachers played a significant role in his career. He studied with former Cleveland Orchestra members Charles Blabolil, Ross Taylor, Milan Yancich (father of Orchestra timpanist Paul Yancich), and Myron Bloom, as well as Marc Fisher of the New York Philharmonic. After earning his bachelor of music degree from Baldwin-Wallace College, he joined the U.S. Military Academy Band at West Point. Mr. Schmitter has also performed with the St. Louis Symphony and the Buffalo Philharmonic.

Mr. Schmitter's experiences on The Cleveland Orchestra's 1965 five-week tour of Russia are particularly memorable. Foreign tours were quite uncommon at that time, and the Soviet audiences were quite receptive and enthusiastic.

He and his wife Wilma have two sons who have experimented with French horn and trumpet, but seem to prefer sports. Mr. Schmitter practices one to two hours a day, teaches at CIM and Akron University, and loves living, working, and bicycling in Cleveland.

Albert Schmitter
Horn
1963

A broken trumpet and a family in which music and jam sessions were a natural part of life led **Richard Solis** to his current position as principal French hornist.

During his early school years, Mr. Solis' trumpet took so long to be repaired that his band director assigned him to the French horn. His later acceptance to CIM, where he studied with former Cleveland Orchestra principal Myron Bloom, confirmed the musical path he would follow.

Mr. Solis never doubted that he would be a professional musician. His grandfather played with a marimba band in vaudeville, his father was a professional bass player, his mother plays piano, and his brother is an ethnomusicologist. Born in Brooklyn, Mr. Solis grew up in Las Vegas where he extended his musical skills in show bands. A versatile musician, he also plays piano, trumpet, jazz bass, and recorder.

Special musical experiences in his life include participating in the Marlboro Music Festival in Vermont and serving as an artist-in-residence at the University of Delaware. A memorable high point was when Pablo Casals called him a "master performer."

Two important nonmusical activities for Mr. Solis are weight lifting and pool, both of which he maintains make him a better musician. "The weight lifting has greatly increased my physical endurance and improved my breathing. I find many similarities between preparing a shot in pool and making an attack on the horn. And, of course, the mental preparation is extremely important."

Richard Solis
Horn
1971

"The Cleveland Orchestra is the only professional orchestra I have ever wanted to play in," states **Ralph Wagnitz**. The dark, German quality of the horn sound appeals to him, and it can be heard in no other American orchestra. In fact, Mr. Wagnitz has spent his entire career with the Orchestra.

He grew up in Northfield Center, Ohio, and began playing the trumpet in the fourth grade. Two years later he volunteered to switch to French horn. However, no horns were immediately available, so he played a mellophone for six months. "The change from trumpet seemed very natural," he recalls. "Perhaps the fact that the mellophone is a right-handed instrument and has piston valves like the trumpet helped the transition."

Mr. Wagnitz had planned a solo career until late in high school when his horn teacher, James Kirk, introduced him to some Dennis Brain recordings. Mr. Wagnitz was almost as excited by the orchestra's performance as he was by the great hornist's. However, it was not until his second year at Ohio State University that Mr. Wagnitz played with an orchestra (his previous work had been with bands). "The first piece we played was the Brahms Symphony No. 4, and I was thrilled. I finally found my niche," he remembers.

Another important turning point in his career was attending the Meadow Brook Festival in 1969. Mr. Wagnitz studied with Arthur Krehbiel, then principal hornist of the Detroit Symphony Orchestra. They worked on orchestral literature and other aspects of ensemble performance. "I learned more in those ten weeks than I had in the ten previous years."

Following his graduation from Ohio State with a bachelor of music performance degree, Mr. Wagnitz enrolled at CIM for one year and worked with former Cleveland Orchestra principal Myron Bloom. Mr. Wagnitz's first association with The Cleveland Orchestra was as sixth horn in a 1972 performance of Mahler's Second Symphony with Eugene Ormandy, a memory which still moves him. He subsequently continued studies with Mr. Bloom, free-lanced, and played as an extra in the Orchestra.

In 1976 he returned to Ohio State and played a season with the Columbus Symphony. Two months after being hired by The Cleveland Orchestra, Mr. Wagnitz was appointed second horn.

Mr. Wagnitz teaches privately. His nonmusical pursuits include hiking, fishing, boating, water skiing, motorcycling, and carpentry.

Ralph Wagnitz
Horn
1977

Bernard Adelstein
Trumpet
1960

A birthday present of a trumpet when he was eight was the start of it all for **Bernard Adelstein**. Lessons followed, and soon the Cleveland native was brought to the attention of Louis Davidson, principal trumpeter of The Cleveland Orchestra.

Mr. Davidson encouraged the young trumpeter at age sixteen to accept the second trumpet position with the Pittsburgh Symphony. The last of the "great tyrants," Fritz Reiner, was his conductor for four years. "At that age, I didn't know he was a tyrant!" comments Mr. Adelstein.

During the summers he also commuted to the Berkshires for further study with Georges Mager of the Boston Symphony Orchestra. Later he worked with Harry Glantz of the NBC Symphony.

Mr. Adelstein left Pittsburgh to serve as principal trumpeter of the Dallas Symphony under Antal Dorati. When Mr. Dorati assumed the post of music director of the Minneapolis Symphony, he took Mr. Adelstein with him as solo trumpeter. Mr. Adelstein remained principal of the Minneapolis Symphony for ten years. During that time he was also on the faculty of the University of Minnesota.

The day he and his family moved into a new house in Minneapolis, Mr. Adelstein received a telegram from George Szell offering him the principal trumpet position of The Cleveland Orchestra. He was elated to become a member of such a magnificent ensemble and particularly remembers Monday morning rehearsals, when the Orchestra "sounded breathtaking on the very first run through the music."

Mr. Adelstein taught at Oberlin for several years and has participated in the Aspen Music Festival and Casals Music Festival, among others. He joined CIM as head of the trumpet department in 1963 and is also chairman of the brass department at the Blossom Festival School. His students play in many orchestras, and he is very proud of those who hold positions in some of the world's leading orchestras.

Mr. Adelstein often has appeared as soloist with The Cleveland Orchestra and is featured on several recordings. He is a member of the Severance Brass Quintet. He usually plays a Bach C trumpet with a lead pipe he designed, which bears his name. When required, he also plays a B-flat, D, E-flat, or piccolo B-flat trumpet, flugelhorn, or posthorn.

Mr. Adelstein practices several hours each day, but takes a few weeks off each summer. "When I return to playing, my approach is much fresher." He also enjoys golf, pocket billiards, jogging, and his sailboat. His brother Rovin plays bass with the Pittsburgh Symphony. His wife Connie is not a musician, but music is important to her and their three children.

Charles Couch is a native Californian who joined The Cleveland Orchestra after a season with La Orquesta Sinfonica del Estado de Mexico in Toluca. He was awarded a B.A. from San Francisco State in 1965, and a master of music degree from Boston University in 1971. His teachers include Donald Reinberg, Roger Voisin, and Orchestra principal Bernard Adelstein.

Mr. Couch, now assistant principal, began studying the trumpet at age eight, playing throughout school in several bands, as well as in the orchestra. A father of three boys, all of whom are musical, Mr. Couch enjoys performing in numerous recitals with his wife Joanne, a soprano. Their performances are mostly of Baroque selections. In addition, Mr. Couch's sister is a professional flutist with the San Diego Symphony and his brother is a professional trombonist.

Mr. Couch enjoys traveling, particularly with the Orchestra's tours. An avid runner for many years, Mr. Couch is the only Orchestra member to have completed a marathon. He frequently runs home from Severance Hall after rehearsals, and logs about twenty-five miles per week.

Charles Couch
Trumpet
1972

James Darling leads a very active artistic life, both as performer and as teacher. Raised in Cincinnati in a family that loved all styles of music and supported his musical endeavors, he began playing the trumpet at age seven. Mr. Darling played trumpet and double bass in high school bands and orchestras, as well as the Junior and Senior Cincinnati Civic Orchestras.

Mr. Darling earned his music degrees from the Universities of Kentucky and Illinois. His teachers included Jack Hyatt, Haskell Sexton, and Adolph Herseth. He was one of four finalists in the Twentieth International Music Competition in Munich. Moreover, he made a successful Carnegie Recital Hall debut; soloed with several orchestras, including the Cincinnati Symphony, Bavarian State Radio Orchestra, Ohio Chamber Orchestra, and University Circle Orchestra; and was a member of a trumpet trio at a Cleveland Orchestra children's Key Concert series. He has also served as principal trumpeter of the Ohio Chamber Orchestra.

A music professor at Baldwin-Wallace Conservatory for fifteen years, Mr. Darling teaches trumpet and chamber music, and conducts the Brass Choir. He is extremely pleased that many of his former students are now in world-class symphonies and on music faculties at several universities. Touring is thus especially enjoyable for Mr. Darling, for it makes possible reunions with former students. Mr. Darling has also taught master classes at six universities. He plays cornet with the Orchestra as well.

A former fiction buff, Mr. Darling now leans toward nonfiction, especially history. "Touring helps one obtain a better perspective on the world, and one becomes more interested in other countries and cultures." At home, he invests much time in family and church activities and is also a photographer.

James Darling
Trumpet
1973

When **David Zauder** came to audition for The Cleveland Orchestra, he planned to stay for one year. He was so impressed with George Szell, the Orchestra, and the uniqueness of Cleveland, that he made the city his home.

Literally ambidextrous, Mr. Zauder leads a double life with the Orchestra. He is a member of the brass section and also Personnel Manager, a post he assumed in 1971, having been Assistant Personnel Manager since 1960. For the past four years he also has been President of the International Orchestra Personnel Managers Conference. He is involved in the future of the symphonic profession because he believes that symphony orchestras have increased in number and have become more accessible and important to the general public. Mr. Zauder would like to ensure that musicians are recognized and rewarded. His role is that of liaison between management, union, and musicians.

A trumpet and cornet player, Mr. Zauder particularly enjoys the cornet because so much beautiful music has been written for it. He played solo cornet with the Leonard Smith Concert Band in Detroit for six years and studied in New York with Harry Glantz and Eric W. G. Leidzen. Before joining The Cleveland Orchestra, he played two seasons as principal trumpeter of the Boston Pops under Arthur Fiedler. Mr. Zauder has been a soloist with The Cleveland Orchestra on several occasions, as well as cornet soloist at the annual Fourth of July Band Concert at Blossom Music Center.

Mr. Zauder has developed and published a trumpet embouchure method that enjoys worldwide acceptance. He is author of many articles and likes working with his dedicated students at CIM.

He received a degree in business administration from Western Reserve University, then continued his studies and became one of the first two students to receive the bachelor of humanities degree from the newly combined Case Western Reserve University.

Mr. Zauder's favorite way to unwind is on the golf course, and his ambition is to play in a pro-am tournament. An active jogger for the past twenty years, Mr. Zauder fondly remembers "Run for Your Life" races he ran from the old University Circle "Y" to downtown Cleveland, the precursors of present-day jogging races through area suburbs.

David Zauder
Trumpet
1958

Robert Boyd
Trombone
1948

Robert Boyd always knew he would be a musician. By age five he was playing the xylophone and later the marimba. The marimba was his primary instrument until, at the age of twenty-three, he became co-principal trombonist of the New York Philharmonic. He began playing trombone in grade school and played in the band through high school. At age fifteen he played first trombone in the Peoria Symphony Orchestra.

He attended the 1939 National Music Camp at Interlochen, Michigan. The orchestra was conducted by a nine-year-old, among others, and they traveled to New York City to play at the World's Fair. Those performances provided Mr. Boyd's first opportunity to play under Lorin Maazel!

Mr. Boyd received the Rochester Prize Scholarship to Eastman. After the U.S. entered World War II, he was engaged as both trombone and marimba soloist of the Navy Band.

After the war he created a marimba show and played in nightclubs and the Capitol Theater in Washington, D.C. He disliked the life, however, and moved to New York. After playing trombone at Radio City Music Hall and on Broadway, and after one year with the Philharmonic, he was engaged as principal trombonist of the Metropolitan Opera Orchestra.

During Mr. Boyd's three years in New York he played with the CBS Symphony, City Center Opera Orchestra, and the Ballets Russes de Monte Carlo and Ballet Theater Orchestras. With his good friend, French hornist Gunther Schuller, he joined Greenwich Village jazz bands after Met performances.

Mr. Boyd still listens to jazz as well as classical orchestral and operatic music. Other activities include teaching at CIM and serious photography. Mr. Boyd plays a King trombone, but also owns a Schlott E-flat trombone, made about 1895, which was purchased by George Szell in Vienna in 1955.

A personal triumph for Mr. Boyd occurred in 1981 when he performed marimba solos with the Blossom Band. Although he had not touched or owned a marimba since 1945, at the urging of the Blossom Band conductor (who had been a shipmate in the Navy Band days), Mr. Boyd purchased a marimba, practiced three hours a day for a year, and was a soloist in the Labor Day concert.

Mr. Boyd believes that Cleveland Orchestra performances have an important effect on listeners' lives. "Our music is a constant in this vale of tears. Here is order, supreme order in a crazy world. If what I do has a small part in enriching someone's existence, it is manna from heaven."

As a young child, **James DeSano** enjoyed listening to his grandfather play the baritone and began playing under his grandfather's instruction, using the solfeggio system and his uncle's trombone. To this day he enjoys both the trombone and the baritone horn and plays the euphonium as well.

Mr. DeSano's high school band director encouraged him to study music education. After being graduated from Ithaca College, he taught elementary and junior high school music for four years. Mr. DeSano played with the Syracuse Symphony and pursued graduate studies at Eastman, where Emory Remington was his most influential teacher. In counseling his own students today, Mr. DeSano encourages them to take a practical approach and combine their musical talents with other skills. Providing a strong example, Mr. DeSano repairs brass instruments and teaches.

He also enjoys performing with the Severance Brass Quintet and the newly formed Cleveland Low Brass Ensemble. A musician who favors Mozart as well as Mahler, he especially likes playing at Blossom Music Center. Mr. DeSano feels he has a special relationship with The Cleveland Orchestra, where he is associate principal, because his peers are "committed musicians, as well as nice people."

The DeSanos, who live in Chesterland, enjoy country living, a luxury within thirty minutes of Severance Hall. As a family they enjoy fishing, hiking, canoeing, and horseback riding. An amateur photographer, Mr. DeSano is the father of three daughters, the youngest of whom now studies percussion and brass.

James DeSano
Trombone
1970

"I look forward to coming to work every day," says **Allen Kofsky**, who plays trombone, bass trumpet, and euphonium for the Orchestra. This Cleveland native, born of Lithuanian parents, has always appreciated music. "When people are happy, they whistle or sing." Mr. Kofsky began lessons at age eight and was a self-motivated, diligent practicer. A junior high school teacher alerted his parents to his talent and suggested he study with John Coffey. He later worked with Merit Dittert. Both were Cleveland Orchestra members, and as a youngster Mr. Kofsky enjoyed attending Severance Hall concerts to watch his teachers. As a teenager he played for the Summer Pops, WGAR staff orchestra, Cleveland Children's Orchestra, and Cleveland Philarmonic.

By a quirk of fate, Mr. Kofsky ended up as a radioman during World War II and found his sense of rhythm a key to learning Morse Code. Following the war and two years of study at CIM, in 1948 he accepted the position of principal trombonist of the Kansas City Philharmonic. In 1955 he returned to Cleveland to join his father's construction business. However, like a good athlete, he kept in training, often substituting in The Cleveland Orchestra and playing at the Hanna Theater, Musicarnival, and Cain Park. Mr. Kofsky eventually returned to the Orchestra full time, at the behest of George Szell.

Since 1975, Mr. Kofsky has served the Orchestra as Assistant Personnel Manager. He attempts to keep at least one full day a week clear for teaching at Baldwin-Wallace College. He encourages his young students who show energy and initiative to be patient, for there is always room for good players in the international music scene. Mr. Kofsky enjoys photography, gardening, and sports. He and his wife Elaine have three children.

Allen Kofsky
Trombone
1961

Edwin Anderson (signature)

Edwin Anderson
Bass Trombone
1964

For **Edwin Anderson**, touring with The Cleveland Orchestra has provided an opportunity to renew old friendships or make new ones among the small, congenial world of symphony trombone players. While stationed with the West Point Band near New York City, he had the opportunity to hear, meet, and study with many of these musicians. These experiences strengthened his desire to make music his profession.

A native New Englander, Mr. Anderson and his wife Virginia enjoy Cleveland for its good schools and huge array of cultural activities, especially in the University Circle area. Their son David is planning a career as a professional bass player, and their daughter Lauren is a violinist. The fact that his children are preparing for careers in music brings Mr. Anderson great satisfaction. "They must have seen how much I have enjoyed orchestral playing," he stated.

A teacher at CIM, he points out that, in addition to great talent, a student must have overwhelming determination in order to succeed in the increasingly competitive world of symphonic music.

Mr. Anderson began playing the bass trombone at age twelve and studied with John Coffey of the Boston Symphony Orchestra, Allan Ostrander and Lewis Van Haney of the New York Philharmonic, and Emory Remington at Eastman. He also studied composition at Eastman with Bernard Rogers. Before joining The Cleveland Orchestra, he played with the orchestras of Buffalo and Rochester. An interview with Mr. Anderson was featured in the *Journal of the International Trombone Association.*

After his public debut on the tuba at the age of ten, **Ronald Bishop** recalls that his instructor noted a resemblance to a well-known book, with a slight variation: "Horn with a Young Man."

Undaunted, Mr. Bishop pursued his musical career and received a bachelor of music degree and performer's certificate from Eastman and a M.S. from the University of Illinois. He has studied with Donald Knaub, Robert Gray, and Chicago Symphony Orchestra member Arnold Jacobs. He has held positions with the Buffalo Philharmonic, American Wind Symphony, San Francisco Symphony Orchestra, and San Francisco Opera Orchestra, but feels that winning the audition for principal tubist of The Cleveland Orchestra was the most satisfying and memorable experience of his musical career.

Mr. Bishop is on the faculties of CIM, Oberlin, and Baldwin-Wallace College and has appeared as soloist with The Cleveland Orchestra on several occasions. In addition to giving numerous recitals and clinics in the U.S., Canada, and the U.K., he has recorded several albums.

Mr. Bishop enjoys performing works of the romantic orchestral literature, such as those of Bruckner, Prokofiev, Strauss, and Wagner. He feels very strongly about the tuba's uniqueness and would like to change its misconceived image as an "oompah" instrument.

A New York state diving champion in college, he almost chose a career in physical education, but his love of music prevailed. Mr. Bishop, his wife Marie, and their son Chris retreat to tiny (½ by 1½ miles) Ruxton Island in British Columbia for their annual vacation.

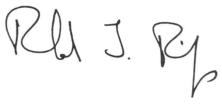

Ronald Bishop
Tuba
1967

Paul Yancich represents the fourth generation of professional musicians in his family. His great-grandfather was a cornet soloist, his grandparents were violinists, and his parents play the French horn. Moreover, his grandfather was assistant conductor of the Rochester Symphony for thirty years, and his father played in the same ensemble. However, his family never pressured him to become a musician. While they were pleased that Mr. Yancich liked music, they encouraged him to pursue other interests.

On his eighth birthday, Mr. Yancich started playing the snare drum. He volunteered to play timpani in the eighth grade, when his orchestra needed someone on that instrument. His first teacher was William Street and he later studied with William Cahn, both of Eastman. Playing was always fun and seemed a natural activity for Mr. Yancich, but he did not begin serious work until he was seventeen and chose a career in music.

At that time, he decided to study with Cloyd Duff at CIM. Many trusted friends had recommended the former Cleveland Orchestra timpanist. Indeed, Mr. Yancich's father had played with The Cleveland Orchestra in 1950 and strongly favored Mr. Duff. As a student at CIM, Mr. Yancich attended every Cleveland Orchestra concert for four years. "Mr. Duff was an excellent teacher and most significant influence on me," he stated. After graduation Mr. Yancich joined the Atlanta Symphony and played there six years.

When Mr. Duff retired, Mr. Yancich returned to Cleveland as the new Cleveland Orchestra principal timpanist. Like his mentor, he also teaches at CIM. In addition, his students come to Cleveland from all parts of the country, and he has been a clinician at several universities.

Mr. Yancich makes his own drumsticks; he has some fifty pairs in the basement of his home. He uses either bamboo or hickory and sews on the felt, recovering one of his eight working pairs every other week. He also enjoys golf, pocket billiards, and spending time with his wife Meg and young daughter Nina.

Paul Yancich
Timpani
1981

Joseph Adato began to study music in New York City at the age of eight, under protest, and was "sometimes forcibly encouraged to practice." He performed at an early age in children's talent shows on radio and television. While he would have preferred playing ball with his peers, Mr. Adato slowly grew to enjoy his musical activities.

In his early teens Mr. Adato played professionally to pay for his lessons and contribute to household expenses. He recalls carrying many pounds of percussion on the New York subway system at all hours of the day and night.

Mr. Adato received his bachelor of music degree from Juilliard. He studied with Morris Goldenberg, whom he credits as being most influential in his musical education. Mr. Adato graduated from Columbia University with a master's degree in music education.

Prior to joining The Cleveland Orchestra, Mr. Adato performed with the New York Philharmonic, the Symphony of the Air, the New York City Center Ballet Orchestra, and the Radio City Music Hall Orchestra. He has served on the faculties of Baldwin-Wallace College and Akron University and currently teaches at Cleveland State University.

While the 1965 Orchestra's tour of the Soviet Union was truly memorable for him, Mr. Adato cites the highlight of all tours as "coming home." The Adatos have three sons, the oldest of whom plays the flute. Mr. Adato's special interests are karate, scuba diving, and weight lifting.

Joseph Adato
Percussion
1962

Robert Matson
Percussion
1952

Robert Matson has been playing percussion since the seventh grade. Although he started playing the piano in the fourth grade, the school band needed a percussionist and Mr. Matson, wanting to join his friends, switched instruments so he could play in the band.

It seems that Mr. Matson has often been "in the right place at the right time" throughout his musical career. After World War II Mr. Matson, stationed in Europe, joined a male chorus in Nice where he coordinated music arrangements and entertained soldiers who were recovering and resting. When he came home to Cleveland, a friend convinced him to tag along to an audition for Juilliard. Mr. Matson auditioned, too, and was accepted, although his friend was not. He studied composition and arranging, as well as percussion. Upon his graduation in 1949, he was hired by the St. Louis Symphony. He stayed in St. Louis until a call from Cleveland with news of a position with the Orchestra brought him home. He serves as the assistant principal timpanist.

Mr. Matson loves all types of music and especially enjoys listening to jazz. One of his most memorable experiences was a Juilliard performance in Carnegie Hall of Bach's *St. John Passion* under Robert Shaw. Mr. Matson's father was deeply involved with community theater in Cleveland and, following this tradition, both he and his wife Mary Ellen have been involved with the East Cleveland Community Theater since its inception over fifteen years ago.

In addition to practicing and performing with the Orchestra, Mr. Matson enjoys playing "commercial" piano, which completes the circle started in the fourth grade.

It is said that many left-handed people gravitate toward the arts. However, the Orchestra reflects average population figures: fewer than ten percent are either left-handed or ambidextrous.

Donald Miller first became interested in percussion instruments after watching a xylophone player on the Ted Mack Show years ago in his home town, Toledo. What Mr. Miller did not know was that that xylophonist was Joseph Adato, with whom he now plays in The Cleveland Orchestra.

Mr. Miller's private teacher in high school, Robert Bell of the Toledo Symphony Orchestra, laid the foundation for his career and urged him to attend Oberlin. Mr. Miller's initial ambition was to become a music educator. However, under the direction of his teacher, Orchestra principal Richard Weiner, Mr. Miller chose a career in performance. He has played with the Toledo Symphony and Casals Festival Orchestras.

Mr. Miller has composed various chamber works and solo pieces and is an editor for a local publishing company. Some of his arrangements have been performed by The Cleveland Orchestra. Currently an adjunct associate professor at Kent State University, Mr. Miller has also taught at Cleveland State University and CIM.

Mr. Miller's nonmusical hobbies include photography and sailing. He, his wife, and their two children appreciate their rural way of life, but Mr. Miller also enjoys his travels abroad with the Orchestra. He has vivid memories of his "first Argentine steak and Salzburger Nockerl."

Donald Miller

Donald Miller
Percussion
1972

Richard Weiner (signature)

Richard Weiner
Percussion
1963

With the support of his family, **Richard Weiner** began to study music at age eight. He was awarded a scholarship to Temple University, studied with Charles Owen, principal percussionist of the Philadelphia Orchestra, and received a B.S. degree. In 1962 he was a scholarship student at the Aspen Festival School and member of the Aspen Festival Orchestra. At Aspen he played solo xylophone in the American premiere of Messiaen's *Oixeaux Exotiques*. Mr. Weiner also played with the Chautauqua Symphony. When George Szell created the principal percussion position in 1968, he appointed Mr. Weiner to that chair.

In 1963 Mr. Weiner received an M.M. with distinction from Indiana University, where he was a percussion student of George Gaber's. He was the first percussionist to receive the University's performer's certificate. He has been on the faculties of the Settlement Music School of Philadelphia, the Philadelphia Board of Education, and Oberlin.

Since 1963 he has taught at CIM and directed the CIM percussion ensemble. His students now play in orchestras such as Cleveland, San Francisco, and the National Symphony, as well as Hollywood studio and contemporary percussion ensembles. He has conducted percussion clinics throughout the U.S. and two symphonic percussion clinics at the 1981 Percussion Arts Society International Convention.

Mr. Weiner has appeared many times as soloist with chamber ensembles. In his earlier Cleveland years he was associated with Donald Erb's music and participated in several recordings and premieres of Erb's works. He also played solo xylophone in the American premiere of Messiaen's *Chronochromie* with the Orchestra in 1967.

Mr. Weiner was principal percussionist on three heralded Telarc digital recordings of the Cleveland Symphonic Winds, conducted by Frederick Fennell. He is also a member of Phi Mu Alpha Sinfonia Honor Society and is presently working on a book on symphonic percussion literature.

In 1976 Mr. Weiner received his juris doctor degree magna cum laude from the John Marshall Law School of Cleveland State University. He has been a member of the Ohio Bar since 1977 and is a practicing attorney. He chaired the Orchestra Committee during the trade agreement negotiations of 1977, 1980, and 1983.

Mr. Weiner has combined his enjoyment of photography with Orchestra tours, five cross-country camping trips, bird-watching, and sailing with his wife Jacqueline and their two daughters.

The Dohnányi name has special significance for **Joela Jones**. At age eleven, after having studied piano for five years with her mother, she spent a summer at Florida State University, where she performed in master classes of Ernst von Dohnányi. Mr. Dohnányi, who impressed her by having known Brahms, identified Miss Jones as a child prodigy. From that time she knew she was destined for a musical career.

A second turning point in Miss Jones' career occurred when she was thirteen and a scholarship student at Eastman. Arthur Fiedler invited her to Boston to play in both the Esplanade and Symphony Hall Pops series. These performances gave her a "marvelous exposure to concerto playing."

The third major step in her career was her first appearance with The Cleveland Orchestra under George Szell, playing the Russell Smith piano concerto. At that time Miss Jones was at CIM. The following year she filled in as keyboard artist for a performance of Stravinsky's *Petrouchka*. In 1972 she became principal of the keyboard section, playing piano, harpsichord, organ, and celesta. A few years later she and first assistant principal Orchestra cellist Richard Weiss were married.

Miss Jones feels she never encountered any obstacles in her career. She attributes her success to hard work and dedication. "Once you have discovered your God-given gift, and everyone has been given a gift, then work hard, never lose sight of your goals or become distracted or discouraged, and always keep yourself in perspective: stay humble!"

Her most memorable conductors are George Szell, Lorin Maazel, and Pierre Boulez, whose musical genius was a great influence. Miss Jones has conducted as well: in school, at a Blossom Festival Forum concert, and with chamber music groups.

She has appeared as soloist with the orchestras of Boston, Chicago, Detroit, Houston, and Philadelphia, and has performed extensively in solo and chamber music recitals. She often gives master classes in conjunction with Orchestra tours, as well as recital tours. "The classes teach me what today's young musicians need to know about music and piano performance." She also is accompanist for The Cleveland Orchestra Chorus and vocal soloists at rehearsals, a position she considers one of the "extra blessings" of her job.

Miss Jones has recorded on the Orion, Musical Heritage Society, and Chamber Recording labels.

Joela Jones
Keyboard Instruments
1972

Eugene Kilinski

Eugene Kilinski
Librarian
1969

Eugene Kilinski spends his days on floors above stage level at Severance Hall. He can be found working in the library, surrounded by music scores, or perhaps conversing in halting French to the latest winner of the Casadesus International Piano Competition in the elegant George Szell Memorial Library.

Mr. Kilinski was born in Chicago, where his Polish father, an opera buff, encouraged him to study the violin. He began at age nine, and by the time he was fifteen was practicing up to four hours a day, thanks to the contagious enthusiasm of an inspiring teacher. However, improper early training convinced him that a youngster will probably not be a virtuoso violinist unless technique is perfected. He earned bachelor's and master's degrees (the latter with a major in violin and minor in musicology) with violin training under Gustave Tinlot from Eastman. He also studied with Michael Wilkmirski and Mischa Mischakoff.

Mr. Kilinski has been a member of the Rochester Philharmonic, Chicago Grant Park Symphony, an opera orchestra in Chicago, and the Boston Pops Tour Orchestra. Toward the end of World War II he played trombone and violin for an armed services band in England and the Continent. He has been a violin soloist with the Rochester Civic Orchestra, the Wiesbaden, Indianapolis, and Mansfield Symphonies, the Cleveland Philharmonic, and at a Cleveland Orchestra Twilight Concert. He continues to play in several independent chamber music groups.

In addition, Mr. Kilinski has taught music at Centenary College, Lawrence College, Butler University, and for twelve years at Case Western Reserve University. Currently, as music librarian, his role is not only to take care of all music used by The Cleveland Orchestra, but also to enter in each player's music all changes made by the conductors.

Such a varied musical career has filled Mr. Kilinski's life with rich memories, from hearing Fritz Kreisler's poetic playing to performing *Aida* and *Faust* under Tullio Serafin. He particularly recalls Leonard Bernstein's marvelous interpretation of Mahler's Second Symphony at Blossom Music Center in 1970.

Mr. Kilinski is keenly interested in travel and has published several articles on that topic, as well as music. He has written short stories, a novel, and a play. His son is also a violinist, and his daughter is a medical student at the University of Florida.

Ronald Whitaker's professional responsibilities are as diverse as his interests. A former trumpet player who earned a bachelor of music degree at the New England Conservatory of Music, he shifted his focus and became assistant librarian for the Minnesota Orchestra upon his graduation.

Mr. Whitaker's first summer job was at the age of fourteen at Tanglewood, where he worked primarily in the music library. He also worked in the orchestra libraries at the New England Conservatory and Boston Symphony Orchestra. After eight years in Cleveland as the Orchestra's head librarian, he enjoys his job more each year.

The Whitaker family was very musical, and early lessons in piano and trumpet, coupled with formal training in later years, have given Mr. Whitaker the vast comprehension of music that is necessary to his work. His responsibilities include meeting with resident and guest conductors several months before their concerts to determine the editions of music to be played. He must then either rent or purchase the necessary orchestral parts.

Before Orchestra rehearsals, Mr. Whitaker makes certain that the appropriate music is in its folder on each musician's stand. After each series of concerts, he collects the folders and replaces their contents with the next set of music.

Mr. Whitaker especially enjoys the Oriental cuisines and their preparation. A special hobby is collecting old 78 r.p.m. recordings. He is fond of legendary conductors such as Koussevitzky and Furtwängler. "Their old recordings are the only way one can hear and enjoy their interpretations," he observes.

Ronald Whitaker
Librarian
1975

Severance Hall has been home to The Cleveland Orchestra since February 5, 1931. Thanks to the generosity of Musical Arts Association president John L. Severance, the building was completed during an era of extreme financial insecurity.

Walker and Weeks were the architects, and Severance Hall harmoniously combines elements of Classical, Art Deco, Georgian, and Egyptian Revival styles. The sixteen-sided exterior is Indiana limestone, and the interior contains many fine materials, including marbles, red jasper, bronze, incised glass, and murals.

In 1958 at the behest of George Szell, the main auditorium was renovated to improve acoustics. Primarily, drapes and carpeting were removed, the proscenium arch was relocated, the stage floor was replaced, and a new shell was constructed. The auditorium's seating capacity is 1,996.

Severance Hall also houses a Green Room, chamber music hall, board room, restaurant, broadcast recording booth, libraries, administrative offices, artists' rooms, and storage areas.

Severance Hall

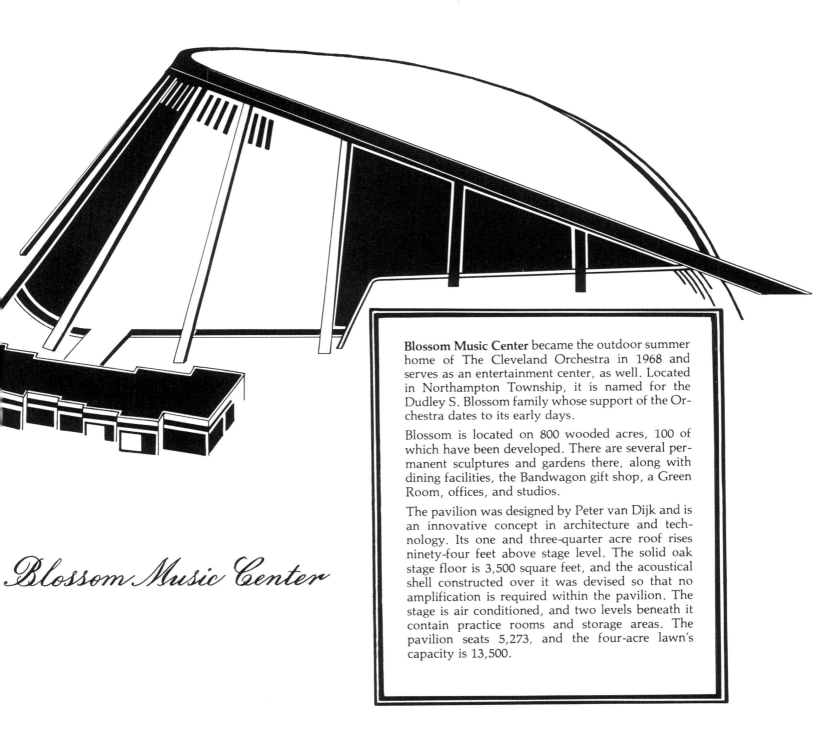

Blossom Music Center

Blossom Music Center became the outdoor summer home of The Cleveland Orchestra in 1968 and serves as an entertainment center, as well. Located in Northampton Township, it is named for the Dudley S. Blossom family whose support of the Orchestra dates to its early days.

Blossom is located on 800 wooded acres, 100 of which have been developed. There are several permanent sculptures and gardens there, along with dining facilities, the Bandwagon gift shop, a Green Room, offices, and studios.

The pavilion was designed by Peter van Dijk and is an innovative concept in architecture and technology. Its one and three-quarter acre roof rises ninety-four feet above stage level. The solid oak stage floor is 3,500 square feet, and the acoustical shell constructed over it was devised so that no amplification is required within the pavilion. The stage is air conditioned, and two levels beneath it contain practice rooms and storage areas. The pavilion seats 5,273, and the four-acre lawn's capacity is 13,500.

Michael Seredick
Assistant Director
Cleveland Orchestra Chorus
1983

Michael Seredick was a "classic late bloomer" when it came to studying music. He started out at Kent State University as an accounting major. He had had some piano lessons, played in a band, and even given keyboard lessons at Halle's. He did not have a sophisticated musical background, "nothing comparable to the experiences I'm giving the kids in my school choir," but his parents imparted to him a respect for music. When he started taking theory and piano electives at Kent State, however, he discovered he was talented and realized he was more interested in music than in numbers. He was twenty-one when he decided to become a music major.

Mr. Seredick earned his B.S. in music education from Kent State in 1967 and his master's in organ in 1976. His full-time job is teaching at Normandy High School, where he directs four choirs daily and also team-teaches a humanities course. He is also organist and choir director at Holy Family Catholic Church in Parma. His first choral experience was with the Oratorio Guild at Kent State.

A member of The Cleveland Orchestra Chorus since 1971, Mr. Seredick's first chance to conduct the Chorus came with ten minutes' notice. During a big snowstorm in 1978, Robert Page called to say he had been delayed and asked for someone to take over the rehearsal until he got there. Mr. Seredick was there. "I was lucky," he related. "It was familiar Christmas repertoire and it was all in English. But if I hadn't been able to take over that night, there were twenty or thirty people who could have."

Now that he is officially the Chorus' assistant director, Mr. Seredick usually has more warning before he leads a rehearsal. When he can plan ahead, he studies Mr. Page's score, which is marked and color-coded to the last detail. Otherwise, Mr. Seredick tries to keep abreast of everything covered in rehearsal, including taking down the markings for every voice part. He has to be prepared to step in at a moment's notice, cover the material, and keep things moving so he does not lose the singers' attention.

"The people in the Chorus are here for three things," Mr. Seredick believes. "They're here for the conductor; they're here for the composer and the work; and they're here to share their talents with The Cleveland Orchestra." He views his challenge as twofold: to win the confidence of his fellow singers and to accomplish something musically. Sometimes though, after spending much of the rehearsal in detail work, he likes to try a run-through. "After I piece out the detail, it's good to shut my mouth and let the music flow from the Chorus."

Cleveland Orchestra Chorus

One hundred eighty men and women, with musical scores and pencils in hand, spend nearly all their Monday evenings from September to May in a large church social hall. They are The Cleveland Orchestra Chorus, and they come from all parts of the greater Cleveland area—some from as far away as Akron, Canton, Mansfield, Elyria, and Orrville—to make music with the Orchestra.

Each Chorus member devotes approximately 225 hours per season to rehearsals and performances of eight or nine different programs, in addition to the demands of a regular job and family obligations. The singers range in age from their late teens to their seventies, and many have been with the Chorus over fifteen years, a few as long as twenty-five. There are many reasons for their devotion, but most cite a love of music, the joy of singing, and the thrill of performing with one of the world's great orchestras.

Though the Chorus is unpaid, its standards are in every respect professional. The majority of members have college educations, though not all were music majors. There are doctors, nurses, lawyers, business people, secretaries, clergymen, full-time homemakers, and teachers of a variety of disciplines.

Many study voice privately, and many perform as soloists in church choirs or other ensembles.

Membership in the Chorus requires a professional level of musicianship. Every singer must reaudition every year. For every missed rehearsal of a given work, a member must prove he or she has learned the material through an individual testing session. Rehearsals are always different due to the varied repertoire, but all rehearsals include solving the musical problems the composition presents, analyzing and dissecting the text, and working toward developing a higher level of vocal proficiency. To encourage continued vocal development, the Chorus sponsors several master classes, available to members at no charge, with the Orchestra's visiting artists. The Chorus also offers voice, solfege, and rhythm classes for a nominal fee.

The Chorus performs in many languages, including English, Latin, German, French, Spanish, Italian, Hebrew, Russian, Hungarian, and Czech. The group must also adapt to various styles, from Baroque polyphony to German Romanticism to French Impressionism to works so avant-garde they are not even written in conventional notation.

Singing in the Cleveland Orchestra Chorus involves a variety of activities. There are regular subscription choral concerts in Severance Hall, along with special programs such as televised concerts, "Choral Masterworks," "The Messiah Sing," the Christmas concert, and the Martin Luther King Memorial concert, which may include another area choir. Cleveland Orchestra Chorus members may also participate in the Blossom Festival Chorus or choose to take the summer off. Almost every year the Chorus performs with the Orchestra in Carnegie Hall.

The group as a whole and many individual members help to promote the Orchestra and support the Musical Arts Association through participation in the annual WCLV Marathon and other volunteer committees. In 1971 the Chorus Operating Committee established the Chorus Endowment Fund, raising over $100,000 primarily through two television specials. The Chorus also earns money from recordings and other services. In addition, the Chorus has attracted handsome gifts of tuxedos for the men and formal attire for the women. All these activities add to the sense of pride Chorus members feel in being a part of The Cleveland Orchestra.

Becky Seredick

Becky Seredick
Director, Cleveland
Orchestra Children's Chorus
1975

A high point in The Cleveland Orchestra's annual Christmas Concert occurs when the **Children's Chorus** performs familiar carols with all the freshness of youth. These sixty children bring a remarkable discipline along with their enthusiasm and clear voices. The person who puts it all together is their director, **Becky Seredick.**

Mrs. Seredick is responsible for preparing the Children's Chorus to perform three or four different programs a year with The Cleveland Orchestra. The conductor on these occasions is usually Robert Page or a guest, but the children do not see him until the week of the performance. At that point they must be ready to rehearse on a professional level along with the Orchestra and the adult chorus. Mrs. Seredick's training gives them the confidence to hold their own and the flexibility to accept the interpretation of a new conductor.

"Obviously, I must begin with a top-notch young-

ster," she observes. Her selection process begins with a letter to every school system in Cuyahoga County, asking each to recommend two children to audition. Girls in the sixth, seventh, and eighth grades are eligible; boys are accepted in the fifth grade because their voices begin to change by the time they reach eighth grade. At that point, their stay in the group is on a week-to-week basis, but a waiting list exists to replace them. The audition itself is rigorous, consisting of a prepared, memorized solo, sight-singing, clapping of rhythmic patterns, ear training, and a sampling of the year's repertoire. Mrs. Seredick listens for a velvety sound, one that is not breathy or nasal. She will take a child who has innate musicianship, even if the voice is not beautiful. Most of the successful applicants have some musical background, either instrumental lessons or Dalcroze. Many are involved in theater and other activities, and most are good students as well. Their parents are extremely supportive.

The Cleveland Orchestra Children's Chorus

The children rehearse two hours per week in the evening until the week of a concert, when they may have rehearsals and performances on as many as six consecutive nights. Mrs. Seredick always starts the rehearsal with a warm-up that may be based on intervals or rhythms that occur in the piece being learned. She then attacks the most difficult parts first. She tries to conduct a piece several ways, so that the children will not be thrown off by a different conductor's style. She keeps things moving quickly and ends with something they like and do well.

Mrs. Seredick is both enthusiastic and demanding. She harps constantly on breath support, rhythm, and diction. She does not tolerate talking or inattention. "It is hard for the new members," she commented, "but they learn to like it. You can't downplay the difficulties, but if you give them quality, they'll come along." She also makes them feel secure by giving lots of praise. They know they have succeeded "when they can go on stage for a performance and do well."

Her favorite conducting assignments are the pops and Christmas concerts. The children often become frustrated with the big orchestral works, because they cannot see how their part fits in. Sometimes though, they are more open to learning new music than adults.

Mrs. Seredick majored in voice at Kent State University and has studied with Melvin Hakola and Faye Liebman Cohen. She taught elementary music for five years before having two children and has recently returned to teaching, with seven classes a day in the Parma School System. She became director of the Children's Chorus in 1975. Mrs. Seredick finds that there are pressures in conducting with a professional group that do not exist at school, but it is a manageable challenge. She hopes still to be conducting when her own daughter is old enough to join the Children's Chorus.

THE CLEVELAND ORCHESTRA

CHRISTOPH VON DOHNÁNYI, music director
Kelvin Smith Family chair

YOEL LEVI, resident conductor

ROBERT PAGE, assistant conductor and director of choruses
Frances P. and Chester C. Bolton chair

CHRISTOPHER WILKINS, conducting assistant
Elizabeth Ring and William Gwinn Mather chair

first violins
Daniel Majeske
concertmaster
Blossom-Lee chair

Eugene Altschuler
*associate
concertmaster*

Yoko Moore
Alvaro deGranda
Ernest Kardos
*assistant
concertmasters*
Erich Eichhorn
Robert Zimmer
Kurt Loebel
Leonard Samuels
Gary Tishkoff
Nathan Snader
Marie Setzer
Boris Chusid
Keiko Furiyoshi
Bert Siegel
Joseph Koch
Stephen Majeske
Lev Polyakin

second violins
Bernhard Goldschmidt
Alfred M. and
Clara T. Rankin chair
Elmer Setzer*
Emilio Llinas†
Vaclav Benkovic
Gino Raffaelli
Carolyn Gadiel Warner
Roberta Strawn
Stephen Warner
Felix Freilich
Samuel Epstein
Richard Voldrich
Joan Siegel
Maurice Wolfson
Vladimir Deninzon
William Brown
Judy Berman

violas
Robert Vernon
Chaillé H. and
Richard B. Tullis chair
Frederick Funkhouser
Edward Ormond*
Muriel Carmen
Ursula Urbaniak Sicre
Lucien Joel
William Kiraly
Arthur Klima
Yarden Faden
Vitold Kushleika
Walter Stummer

violoncellos
Stephen Geber
Louis D. Beaumont chair
Diane Mather†
Richard Weiss*
Robert Perry
Gary Stucka
Jorge Sicre
Catharina Meints
Ralph Curry
Harvey Wolfe
Donald White
Thomas Mansbacher
Martin Simon

basses
Lawrence Angell
Clarence T. Reinberger chair
Anthony Knight†
Scott Haigh*
Jacques Posell
Ethan Connor
Mark Atherton
Harry Barnoff
Martin Flowerman
Thomas Sepulveda

harps
Lisa Wellbaum
Alice Chalifoux chair
Laura Okuniewski†

flutes
Jeffrey Khaner
Elizabeth M. and
William C. Treuhaft chair
Martha Aarons
John Rautenberg††

piccolo
William Hebert

oboes
John Mack
Edith S. Taplin chair
Elizabeth Camus
Pamela Pecha Woods†

english horn
Felix Kraus

clarinets
Franklin Cohen
Robert Marcellus chair
Theodore Johnson
Thomas Peterson†

e flat clarinet
Theodore Johnson

bass clarinet
Alfred Zetzer

saxophone
Thomas Peterson

bassoons
George Goslee
Louise Harkness Ingalls chair
Phillip Austin
Ronald Phillips†

contra-bassoon
Stanley Maret

horns
Richard Solis
George Szell memorial chair
David Glasser†
Ralph Wagnitz
Albert Schmitter
Jeffrey Powers

trumpets
Bernard Adelstein
Richard S. and Robert C. Weiskopf chair
David Zauder
Charles Allan Couch†
James Darling

cornets
David Zauder
James Darling

trombones
Robert Boyd
Gilbert W. and Louise I. Humphrey chair
Allen Kofsky
James DeSano††

bass trombone
Edwin Anderson

euphonium and bass trumpet
Allen Kofsky

tuba
Ronald Bishop
Nathalie C. Spence and
Nathalie S. Boswell chair

timpani
Paul Yancich
Otto G. and Corinne T. Voss chair
Robert Matson†

percussion
Richard Weiner
Margaret Allen Ireland chair
Joseph Adato
Robert Matson
Donald Miller

keyboard instruments
Joela Jones
Rudolf Serkin chair

librarians
Ronald Whitaker
Eugene Kilinski
Joseph Koch
Robert Zimmer

personnel manager
David Zauder
Allen Kofsky
assistant

*First Assistant Principal
†Assistant Principal
††Associate Principal